PUT THE
KETTLE ON
THE IRISH LOVE AFFAIR
WITH TEA

JUANITA BROWNE is a Zoology graduate who migrated into print media and television after college. She published her first book, *Ireland's Mammals*, in 2005. Besides wildlife, one of the other great loves of her life is a nice cup of tea. Neither a tea addict nor a tea connoisseur, she simply enjoys plain old Irish tea and, most importantly, the chat that goes with it. And this is what this book is about.

Juanita would love to hear your tea stories:
teaireland@gmail.com and on Twitter @bookoftae

TO MY MOTHER, WHO TAUGHT
US ABOUT KINDNESS,
LISTENING AND HOSPITALITY,
AND THE THERAPY TO BE FOUND
IN A CUP OF TEA AND A CHAT.

PUT THE KETTLE ON

THE IRISH LOVE AFFAIR WITH TEA

Juanita Browne

To one of our own,
even if only by marriage!

Best wishes,

Juanita Browne

The Collins Press

FIRST PUBLISHED IN 2013 by
The Collins Press
West Link Park
Doughcloyne
Wilton
Cork

© Juanita Browne 2013

A CIP record for this book is available from the British Library.

ISBN: 978-184889-187-6

Design and typesetting by Burns Design
Typeset in Rotis
Printed in Poland by Białostockie Zakłady Graficzne SA

Photographs courtesy the author unless otherwise credited.
Photographs on pp viii (from top left, photos 1, 6, 7, 8 and 11), 7, 46
and 83 courtesy SXC.

Cover photographs
Front and spine: The O'Connor Family, Clonea (O'CONNOR FAMILY)
Back (top, l–r) Patrick McDonnell (DAVID McDONNELL), Imelda Byrne, Mick
Gurley (GER TREHY), Mary McEvoy; (bottom, l–r): Ann Stone, Tom Dunne
(JESSICA KELLY), Róisín O, The Clancy Brothers and Tommy Makem, 1964
(INDEPENDENT NEWSPAPERS IRELAND)

CONTENTS

ACKNOWLEDGEMENTS

I must thank all of the people who welcomed me into their homes and their places of work and took time out of their lives to meet a stranger (who they could only assume was crazy) to talk about tea. It's hard to believe anyone said yes, and not only that, but everyone was so friendly and welcoming. The experience would renew one's faith in Irish hospitality and kindness.

Amazingly, everyone had something different to say! I remember Stephen McCahill questioned the feasibility of 'getting a whole book out of tea', and suggested perhaps a short story instead. Of course, this was before he proceeded to talk for three hours about tea, along with the lovely John Joe McBrearty, in his pub in Ardara, County Donegal. It was only when people thought about it that it stirred so much opinion, nostalgia and stories.

It was a real privilege to hear about people's personal lives and family histories. I gained access to the inner sanctum of Dungarvan Men's Shed, where by rights no woman should ever set foot. Matt Jordan guided me around his treasure trove of teapots in Roscommon. I gatecrashed Kathleen and Des's wonderful card game in Manor Kilbride, County Wicklow, a bowls match at Brownstown Bowls Club, and was invited to take tea with the lovely ladies of Trim ALPS.

I also have to mention all the tea and biscuits, cakes and buns I was offered while we talked tea. Thank you to John McAreavey and his lovely parents, Brendan and Latitia – to be welcomed into people's homes was very special and humbling. The Irish welcome is alive and well. Not only did people agree to be quizzed and recorded and photographed, they also offered up further interviewees and songs, much more than I could fit between these covers. On top of talking about tea, they often relayed their own captivating life stories.

Sincere thanks to Cepa Giblin, Seamus Connolly, Maria O'Hara, Niamh Shaw, John Fardy, Jean McEvoy, Mag Malone, Aiveen Kemp, Mick Gurley, Maria Dowling, Eddie Bennett, Roisín O'Sullivan, Eamon Dallett, Olivia Kelly, Judith Browne, Mary Leenane and Hannah Quigley who put me in contact with so many great contributors. Thank you to Michael Hinch from Independent Newspapers who so kindly helped me to source wonderful old photographs of tea drinkers. Special thanks to Denis Daly.

To all of my wonderful friends – in Ireland, Australia, Japan, Belgium and Scotland; how lucky I am to have so many great friends who happen to be brilliant storytellers and writers!

To Dominic Timpson who went above and beyond the call of tea duty, thank you. A special mention must go to my lovely sister Aisling, who helped with typing and, more importantly, with her enthusiasm and faith in the idea from the very beginning. I'm only sorry that she says she can no longer enjoy a cup of tea without analysing it.

To my husband Joe and my lovely boys Ben and John, I love you very much, and look forward to many cups of tea with you in the future.

Thank you so, so much to all the interviewees and writers whose stories appear in the following pages. Because so many tea lovers were willing to take part in this strange project, we couldn't fit everyone in this book, but hopefully we will see the rest of you in *Put the Kettle On Again*! It truly was a privilege to meet you all and an honour to facilitate the telling of your stories. I'm definitely the better for hearing them.

JUANITA
teaireland@gmail.com

INTRODUCTION

I n the ward of a maternity hospital, a baby boy takes his first breaths in this strange new world, while his mother rewards herself with a cup of tea. A Holy Communion group retires to a parish hall for tea and cakes. A Gaelic football team wins a match and the team and supporters troop to the clubhouse to a spread of tea and sandwiches. A big mug of tea rests on the student's desk as he crams for his Junior Cert. A teenage boy sits down with his parents to tell them his girlfriend is pregnant: they quickly put on the kettle. A couple queue up in Dublin Airport before their flight to the sun, and she checks that she remembered to pack the teabags. On Valentine's Day he brings her breakfast in bed, with her tea made just as she likes it. A woman climbs to the top of Mount Brandon and, while admiring the view, she reaches into her backpack for her flask of tea. In the office canteen, stories are told and business is done while the kettle boils. A woman dies in hospital and a cup of tea is placed in her husband's trembling hands. At the wake, the kettle will be constantly on the boil for the mourners. Tea is a feature of the everyday, but it is also the backdrop to some of our most life-changing events. A drink to wake you up and to calm you down, a drink to warm you up and even to cool you down, tea is used for celebration, for consolation, to quench thirst. This is a book about a very Irish cup of tae.

Over the course of this project, many people asked how I came to begin writing a book about tea. It's a good question. I guess I love tea myself, and I have always been aware of how particular people are about their tea, and how important it is to us. I remember working as production secretary on a television programme called the *Gay Byrne Music Show* during a stint in RTÉ after college. I remember as a 22-year-old newbie the first night of the show, worrying about whether the running order had been distributed correctly to all the crew and whether the audience seating had all gone to plan. I hadn't foreseen

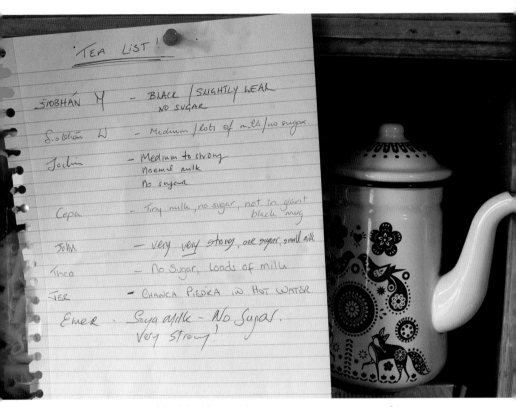

The 'Tea List'. Photograph by John Murray, who never ever says no to a cup of tea.

the only problem being the late availability of tea in the green room. When one of the star guests, Ronnie Drew, came to me looking for his tea, I had to explain that the tea trolley hadn't yet arrived from the canteen and thankfully he was very nice about it. But it was amazing to see an Irish music legend so in need of his cup of tea before the show!

Then, a few years ago, I started working on a wildlife documentary project with Crossing the Line Films, a film production company based in Wicklow. I noticed a sign on the wall of the kitchen, over the kettle, that listed the tea-making instructions for each staff member. No matter who volunteered to make the tea, the 'Tea List' ensured that everyone got the cup they wanted. The correct tea was so important that the list was created to leave no room for human error.

It was this list that planted the seed for a book about tea, because everyone knows a tea addict, a tea-leaf 'snob', someone who likes tea so strong 'you wouldn't need faith to walk on it', or someone so fussy you'd prefer not to make it for them. And I began to wonder why tea is so important to Irish people and about all the social situations that call for tea and what memories might be stirred by talk of tea. Everywhere I went, somebody started talking about tea and the 'proper' way to make it. So I began to ask people about their tea drinking, their 'rules' for the perfect cup, and their most memorable cups, for better or worse. What emerged were intriguing tales of Irish life and insights into human nature, because, after all, 'my cup of tea' is not your cup of tea. It is the most personal of choices.

The Irish are officially the biggest tea drinkers on the planet. Many of us drink six to seven cups a day, the equivalent of 7 lb of dry tea leaves each year. Today, on this small island, the kettles were put on, favourite drinking vessels selected, and about 20 million cups of tea were brewed to just the right strength; milk and sugar measured out in just the right quantities; and our favourite brew enjoyed by young and old, from all walks of life – in homes, hospitals, prisons, schools, farms, offices, factories, fire stations, galleries, football stadiums, and cafés.

We look to tea as part of the solution to every Irish dilemma. It is consumed in bulk at ICA meetings, Mother and Toddler mornings, business meetings, after computer classes or donating blood. Tea is truly our national drink.

The ritual of making tea accompanies both joyous and tragic events in our lives, but it is automatic, we don't even think about it. It is also part and parcel of the Irish welcome to offer tea to a guest, and when none is offered it can cause huge offence. We remember how our loved ones take their tea, and it is touching to hear someone describe exactly how a parent liked their tea, despite their passing decades before.

Tea has become part of our make-up and living memory. Tea advertisements engender nostalgia for simpler times – most of us would recognise the jingle, 'Extra quality, extra flavour, Lyons the quality tea'. Everyone remembers the Lyons minstrels dancing across our television screens and the prize cars promised in every pack. We can visualise the TV stars that were the PG Tips chimpanzees, while Barry's offered us those 'Golden Moments' of sharing a cuppa with a loved one, or enjoying a mug of home on the other side of the world, or even that precious moment when you receive a new teabag from your groom-to-be! The Mrs Doyle character in the TV comedy series *Father Ted* became an Irish icon, partly due to her tea-pushing approach so familiar to every Irish person.

Each contributor has provided something new to the Irish tea story. Author Denyse Woods explores the growing of tea plants in Africa and India and the lengthy journey to Irish mugs and the shame of a poorly prepared cup of tea. Many contributors remember the tea rationing during the Second World War, while others recall tea enjoyed from the billycan, while cutting turf on the bog. On a building site, we meet a builder who recalls the 'tea boy' who was a feature of every building site in the country until the 1980s. We hear how important the tea break is for farmers and wildlife cameramen, working outside in all types of Irish weather. We learn the extent of the underground export of Irish teabags in personal suitcases passing through Dublin Airport, and in packages carried by An Post airmail to Irish emigrants all around the globe.

'Talking tea' with people also revealed the changes in our lifestyles and living conditions over the years. Contributors recall fetching water from outdoor wells, the arrival of electricity, and getting milk for their tea from their own cow or goat, highlighting how convenient everything has become. A teacher revealed that toddlers today no longer know the word 'saucer' as so many people use mugs, so some of the ritual and etiquette of serving tea has now disappeared.

Tea habits also reflect the variety of traditions in different parts of the country. For example, in north Donegal, a wake is still a tea-only three-day event in the bereaved family's home, which is referred to as the 'corp-house'. At times of stress, as many interviewees have noted, making tea may simply give us something tangible to focus on. I suppose there's comfort in the fact that when you're in control of nothing else in your life, at least you can make a cup of tea the way you like it.

It was also clear that in north Donegal, and on the Mullet Peninsula, everyone still knows their neighbours and, as in many rural areas, people still call to each other's homes – unexpectedly – for tea, while in Kildare it has become more common to phone or text first to make an appointment. In urban areas like Dublin, people are living more independent lives, and may not even know their neighbours. Some contributors mentioned how they now talk to friends in Australia, via the Internet, more often than they would their next-door neighbours. I consider this a great pity – that the closeness and spontaneity that once defined Irish society has dissipated. What a pity it would be if we lost that Irish habit of dropping into each other's homes for a cuppa.

Tea may seem a strange topic for a book. But what other everyday event – besides our Irish weather – generates so much conversation and opinion? It punctuates the day for so many of us. It is the oil to conversation and storytelling and the sharing of news, all so important to the Irish psyche. This book is an anthology of conversations about tea. I hope you get as much enjoyment as I did from meeting all of the contributors to this book as they discuss this surprisingly essential part of their life.

The Birth of Tea

According to legend, the story of tea began in China in 2737 BC.
The Chinese emperor Shen Nung, a famous herbalist, worshipped
for discovering the medicinal properties of many plants, always
drank boiled water. One day, Shen Nung was sitting under a tree,
a tree now known as 'Camellia sinensis'.

A wind of change was blowing. His servant was boiling drinking
water for the emperor when some leaves fell from the tree, into the
boiling water. Shen Nung decided to try this accidental
infusion and he thought it was delicious.

Perhaps Shen Nung slurped his tea, let out a long sigh and
exclaimed to his servant ' Ah, that's a grand cup of tae.'

EDDIE CANTWELL

Eddie Cantwell is a local historian living in the parish of Abbeyside, Dungarvan, County Waterford. A former President of Waterford County Museum, Eddie has published two books on local family history from the 1800s.

COURTESY MAY CANTWELL

'Throw the kettle on and we'll make a cup of tea,' said my great grandmother, and I reluctantly released my hold on the fire machine, allowing it to spin slowly down. I was 'blowing the fire' and now that the firewood and coal were crackling, I wrestled the big kettle from the crane which hung over the open fire and dragged it to the bucket of water. There was no tap water in the cottages back then, in the early 1950s. A pump that served the community was located a half mile from the cottage. The kettle was 'as black as the hobs of hell' from years' hanging over the open fire. When the water started to bubble out over the spout, it was time to 'give the teapot a scald, like a good man.' Putting tea leaves into a pot without first administering a scalding was considered an unforgivable error. The boiling water must be poured into the teapot, the cover replaced and the pot given a good swirl before dumping the contents.

The tea was measured according to the number of people partaking of the wonderful brew. The teapot was then placed on the hot ashes for a few minutes to 'draw' while the table was set with milk and sugar. The drinking of tea was accompanied by great slices of homemade bread, thickly coated with butter, which was made by the local nuns at Carriglea Convent.

The fire was continually on the go in my great grandmother's house and the kettle bubbling on the crane. Visitors continually dropped in and this was always an excuse for the making of tea.

Tea purchased in Dungarvan was weighed out on scales which stood on the shop counter; it was scooped up from a large bin or a 'tea chest' by the shop owner and placed in a strong brown paper bag. Tea chests were a sought-after commodity by young married couples. They were then used to contain young children who might easily wander into the open fire while the mother was busy at household chores.

That's a great cup of tae entirely, sure you could stand on it

According to the menfolk who visited the house, 'You can't bate tae from an open fire.' They enthused, 'God, Kate, but that's a great cup of tae entirely, sure you could stand on it.' Tea made from the open fire had a certain flavour which came from the smoke off the burning timber. This too was the flavour favoured by council workers who were acclimatised to the tea made in their Tommy cans, from water boiled on the side of the road over a makeshift fire.

Eddie's granddaughter, Nzera Tara Cantwell, 'blowing the fire' in Eddie's neighbour's house in 1998.

COURTESY EDDIE CANTWELL

Tea at the headland, at the Foley farm, Ballinacourty, Dungarvan, County Waterford, 1960s. Michael Foley in centre.
COURTESY JOHN FOLEY

My grandfather drank tea from the saucer, spilling it from the cup and slurping great draughts of it. I never saw him drinking directly from the cup. My great aunt Hannah was often called on to read the tea leaves which sat thick at the bottom of the cup. Giving the cup a little shake, she drained the leavings and carefully studied the contents before proclaiming prophesies of an unbelievable nature. She refused to read the tea leaves for us youngsters.

In later years, the art of tea making became more sophisticated when the copper electric kettle was introduced into the household. This generated a great deal of interest from neighbouring women who dropped by to see the electric kettle in operation and sample tea from such a device. But ... 'you can't bate tae from an open fire'.

As youths during our school summer holidays in the early 1960s, a number of us worked for the farmers at Ballinacourty, in Dungarvan. I have many memories associated with tea drinking from this period. The arrival of tea in the field was keenly anticipated and offered a welcome break from some back-breaking task. Sweet gallons were sought-after receptacles for transporting tea to the field and an order had to be placed with shop owners well in advance if one was required. These were also used for milk which was delivered to the door and measured into the gallon back then, and indeed for fetching water from the pump.

Tea stayed very hot in the gallon. Great chunks of bread, with lashings of butter, accompanied a big mug of sweet tea, and there was nothing to compare with sitting down on a headland and enjoying this particular form of recreation.

Some of the farmhouses made very weak tea and a number of us youths met up in the evenings to discuss the events of the day and, of course, to compare the hospitality of the farmhouse. Was the dinner good? What was the tea like? One lad was famously noted for exclaiming: 'I had duck for dinner – duck in and duck out, and tea like piss.' But on the whole, Ballinacourty farmers served the very best. I can certainly attest to that.

Some families had trouble with teacups. They kept getting dropped and parents just got fed up replacing them. A great quantity of jam was used with bread and butter in those days so the good old jam jar was adopted; all children in the house had their own private jam jar. A coloured thread was tied around the neck of each jar for identification. A spoon was first placed in the jar before the tea was poured to avoid cracking it. Drinking from a jam jar was difficult (I know, I tried it) because the jar was very hot and burned the hand. The other problem was when it was raised high, the tea leaves came with the tea and you ended up with a mouthful of tea leaves!

Another method of tea drinking favoured by the factory workers at Dungarvan Leather factory was drinking tea from milk bottles. There

Sam and Tommy enjoying a cup of tea at Dungarvan Leather Factory, 1980s.
COURTESY EUGENE COLLINS

The O'Connor family enjoying a cup of tea at the headland, Clonea, County Waterford, 1952. COURTESY THE O'CONNOR FAMILY

were two reasons for this. It kept the tea hot for much longer and after the tea break was over, the bottle was taken to the work place and sipped regularly. One such tea drinker was Johnny. His tea bottle stood like a statue on a shelf by his machine. He was close to the canteen and kept it replenished. This practice eventually attracted the attention of the Managing Director who approached Johnny and addressed him so: 'here, my man, you seem to be drinking tea all day every day. I wonder if you are aware of company policy regarding tea breaks?' Johnny was quick to ward off any attack on his tea drinking: 'Of course I am, Mister O'B, but I'm under doctor's orders.'

DYLAN LABUSCHAGNE

Dylan Labuschagne, aged 4¾, just before he started school in Ballysax National School, The Curragh, County Kildare.

Dylan likes to dunk his biscuits in tea. Curious about the drink in his mother's mug – something he was always warned away from because of the risk of getting scalded – he was finally allowed to dunk a biscuit and taste it for the first time. He loved it!

Now he has progressed to drinking the odd cup of milky tea, complete with a biscuit or two. Dylan's favourite mug is a Mickey Mouse one, the biggest one in the house.

TOM DUNNE

Tom Dunne is a radio broadcaster and lead singer with Something Happens.

COURTESY JESSICA KELLY

How do you take your tea?
Strong, with lots of milk (no sugar since Lent 1970), and preferably early in the morning. Tea seems to lose potency as the day progresses.

How many cups per day?
As many as possible: weekdays, away from prying eyes, easily five or six. Weekends, in the bosom of my caffeine-obsessed family, a maximum of two. But the two at the weekend are the nicest ones.

Do you have a favourite brand?
No and that causes some fights! I can detect differences from one brand to the next, but I find once you open a box you get used to it and love it.

Do you take Irish teabags abroad with you?
Only if I was going away for a very long time. After about a week of painful American teabags with strings on little bags, a box of Lyons can become more desirable than a night out with Salma Hayek.

When did you start drinking tea?
Probably before I was weaned. I think my parents believed tea was the missing link between breast and solids. I can remember drinking it from those spill-proof mugs you give to toddlers, but they were very health conscious – only about six heaped spoons of sugar in it.

What was your best cup of tea?
Tea is always about time and place: anyone who has ever had a baby will tell you about the post-delivery tea and toast. So I can confidently say the best cup I ever had was 12 July 2006 at about 8 p.m. That was bliss. But since that pivotal moment, the best tea moment of the week is every Saturday morning at about 7.30 a.m. I get up with the kids and as they cause mayhem, I have a cup of tea with a slice of sourdough toast. It is a combination that easily takes the sting out of the early hour. I make a second mug as I start drinking the first.

Do you have a favourite cup?
Yes, it was a present from Sean Moncrieff's wife. It says 'TOM' on it and is black with little stars and a moon, and an orange interior. Need I say more? Followed closely by a Manchester United one that says 'Beckham'. It was my lucky mug during the treble winning season of 1999, but I threw it out after a run of bad results in 2005.

Would you drink tea at a Something Happens gig?
No one drinks tea at gigs. No one. If a member of my band was caught drinking tea at a gig, he would quite rightly be asked to leave.

No one drinks tea at gigs.

Why do Irish people love tea so much?
When you are weaned on it, it can be hard to give up. We are a nation of worriers, and in the middle of a good long fret, there is nothing more reassuring than a nice cup of tea.

MARIA DOWLING

Maria Dowling is a counsellor and psychotherapist, working in a private practice in Sutton, Dublin. She is married to Karl and has three children.

Maria and Stephanie Dowling enjoying 'tea time'.
COURTESY SEÁN DOWLING

I work in counselling and psychotherapy and I can honestly say that tea drinking played a part in my coming into this work. I deal with trauma a lot and inevitably I get asked what brought me into such a difficult profession. Questions like that have made me wonder about my journey into the work and what I think is valuable about human relating.

My mother is a wonderfully compassionate woman, with an easy personality and quick wit. Growing up, I recall our kitchen being such a busy place, with people constantly coming and going. Our back door and back garden gate were always open. I would often come in from school and find a neighbour sitting in the little seat by the open fire, sipping tea and waiting on my mother to resume a much-interrupted conversation. Often people sat in that chair, a cup in their hand, and I knew that they were suffering. I also knew that they were comforted sitting there. Tea was the key. If the kettle went on and a cup was handed to them, then my mother was available to listen. It was like the cup of tea was the message that they were welcome and we all read it as such. If a caller was not offered tea, then time for talking was not available.

I can honestly say that my mother ministered to many in that small kitchen over decades and it had a big impact on me. She would often tip us off that someone had received very bad news and would we just 'take a moment to say hello'. I came to realise the value of simply giving time and attention to someone. Often we don't have much wisdom to offer, but if we have time and heart, much good is done. For me, to this day, I associate giving tea with the offer of time, kindness and a listening ear.

In psychotherapy, boundaries between the client and therapist are crucial to the work. It's a professional relationship and one that will end some day. Much happens within it and both parties experience deep connection in the healing process. I measure my use of offering a client tea, but have had occasions where I know its impact was profoundly positive. There have been some occasions where to not offer a cup of tea with sugar would be wrong. In these unique situations, the power of this little brew has always amazed me. It is so packed with meaning: a sense of comfort and care and a salve to a body unable to help itself. When people are vulnerable or frightened, a cup of tea is not only physically soothing, but helps with self-consciousness. Much is evident in how someone holds their cup, toys with it, caresses it and feels its heat. For those difficult sessions, it appears that the cup becomes the focus for the distress and it enables them to talk. Many who sat with my mother didn't say much, they just held their cup, and as a young person I read them by what they did with it.

My mother is actively involved with our family life and often watches us running around from one extra-curricular activity with our kids to another, trying to be good parents. Every now and again, she simply tells me that the best thing I can give my kids is my time. This always makes me think. Something we therapists watch is how much relational and connection energy we put into the work and how much we have left over for our family and friends. As the mother of young children, I have to be mindful of how much of myself I have to offer my kids, especially after a tough week.

I have a little girl and our connection time is 'tea time'. Girls seem more open to just sitting and talking. My boys tend to talk to me in the context of an activity. My Stephanie is like me; she likes pretty things. I have a china tea set with red roses and delicate cups. I love it. My mother gave it to me when I got married. It had been given to her many years before and it's one of my treasures. I also have my grandmother's tea set from when I was a child. She taught me so much about the value of tea time. She loved to make tea time special. When I look at those old cups, I remember happy times, where everyone had a special place at the table set for them, adults and children. To this day, I study the cup I am handed. I don't like bulky mugs. I'm a bit odd on this. My husband has often had the tea he's offered me rejected, as I search the cupboard for the cup I want. I also like the tea to fill just over half the cup. I like topping up. I love teapots, with their S-shaped spouts and how they pour. I love the feeling inside when someone offers to top up a cup of tea. It's like more time is on offer; we don't have to stop being together yet.

Stephanie and I have tea time once a week. Sometimes we go out and have tea and talk. Sometimes, I just don't have the time for this, so I set a small table in my home office. I take out my rose tea set, with scones and napkins and we get to have 'girl talk'. It is so enjoyable and I know it is the stuff of memories. It helps me too with my work guilt. I can console myself that I know this child, have given her my undivided attention and know what is happening in her world. I can honestly say that we are closer as a result of this little ritual.

Anyone who pauses to reflect on their relationship with tea will probably discover, as I have, that memories are evoked where we can almost breathe in the atmosphere of times gone by. These memories are 'infused' with meaning for me, as I can remember how I formulated my thinking on what matters in life.

We Irish don't celebrate tea for what it has given us. It remains obscure, yet vital in most households today. My family never 'took' to coffee, so I do wonder what the 'order of ordinary life' would have been had there been no tea over the decades. Truthfully, I can't imagine.

The Clancy brothers and Tommy Makem having a cup of tea before they go onstage, 1964.

ROSITA AGNEW

Rosita Agnew comes from Carrickmacross, County Monaghan. She has worked for the European Union since 2000 and lives with her husband Stuart and son Liam in Brussels.

Rosita at the Atomium, one of Brussels' great landmarks.
COURTESY STUART HICKEY

It's quite possible I would have my Irish passport revoked if the Tea Gardaí were to inspect how I make tea. A friend who witnessed the process said that I might as well just wave the teabag over the cup. The teabag in fact gets the quickest dip. I also add the milk first because I hate to waste time and like to have everything ready (biscuits chosen, etc.) by the time the kettle is boiled. So it starts off looking like milk and water and ends up looking like milk and water. In fact, I once forgot to put the teabag in and only realised when I was halfway through drinking it! I also drink decaffeinated tea. I started when I was pregnant (Liam is now two years old) and never bothered changing as I honestly can't taste the difference, and surely unleaded must be better for you?

I'm certain that my mother is responsible for my addiction to weak tea. One of my earliest memories (not the earliest, which is of my dad flushing my dummy down the toilet!) is the two of us sitting at the kitchen counter together after the others had been packed off to school and before my brother had arrived on the scene. I would, like any child, insist on having what she was having, but mine

My mother is responsible for my addiction to weak tea

had to be of a weaker variety. I also vaguely remember that every so often she would let me eat a spoonful of sugar, but I think we were supposed to keep that one to ourselves ...

I am, of course, banned from making tea when I return home to Carrickmacross (I live in Belgium). My dad explains that his family used to make the tea, say the rosary, and then drink the tea, meaning that his is obviously of a much stronger variety. My husband's grandmother used to say about such tea: 'You could trot a mouse on that.' My husband also likes what you might call 'proper tea', so I make his and then recycle his teabag for my cup (Carrickmacross is dangerously close to the Cavan border).

My husband is the only other person on the planet who can make tea for me (I'm hoping that if he reads this, he will feel qualified to do it even more often). All others, despite their most sincere attempts, make tea the way they like to drink it. Don't we all?

I drink litres of tea at a time – the capacity of the mug I drink from is a half litre so that's the sort of quantity we're talking about. Maybe four or five mega-mugs a day.

Living in Belgium makes me realise that drinking tea with milk (à la Barry's and Lyons or 'builders' tea') is a strictly non-Continental European thing to do. Over here, people drink 'infusions', what we call herbal tea. And lots and lots of coffee. In fact, in restaurants and cafés here, the hot water for tea usually comes from the coffee machine and not a kettle so it is never properly boiling. There is also no such thing as scalding the teapot or the cup which means that when an Irish person orders tea 'out', they are inevitably sorely disappointed. I guess in Ireland drinking tea had a lot to do with keeping warm which is why tepid tea never really does the trick for us. What's more, the teabags over here are of terrible quality – my sister's take on this is that they brush the floor in the teabag factory, look in the dustpan and say 'that'll do for the Continent.'

Naturally, we ensure a steady import of Irish teabags. Each Irish visitor, in order to qualify for entry to our home, must bring some. Rashers and sausages are optional!

TOM McDONALD

Tom McDonald is a plasterer from Newbridge, County Kildare.

I first drank tea as a child with my mother – she used to put the tea into my little baby bottle. You wouldn't see it now but years ago it was common to put the tea with milk and sugar into the baby's bottle. I still take it the same way – the milk and sugar, but I gave up the bottle, I use the cup now.

I drink four or five cups of tea a day. I love the tea, especially first thing in the morning. I used to smoke, and the first thing I used to have was a cup of tea and a fag and then I'd drink tea again at half ten, one o'clock. It's a pick-me-up. It's great and it gives you a few minutes to relax. Some people drink coffee, but I never liked it. I actually married a woman whose maiden name is Coffey, so I could never drink coffee after that.

The best cup of tea is after – how could I put it – after you'd be bonding with your wife, I can't go into too much detail, but when you'd be after bonding with your wife, it's grand to sit up in the bed and have a cup of tea and you just sit back and relax.

I do have a favourite mug. The grandchildren bought me a big granddad's mug and it fits about three cups of tea. It's great because the first cup of tea is the best cup of tea, the second cup isn't as nice – so if you get all the tea into the cup at the one time, it's far nicer.

When we used to go to the bog as kids, years ago, your mammy would put all the tea, milk and sugar in a big lemonade bottle and wrap it up in a towel to keep it warm and you'd drink the tea in the bog when you'd be cutting the turf because you had no water or nothing

Your mammy would put all the tea, milk and sugar in a big lemonade bottle and wrap it up in a towel to keep it warm

down in the bog and you'd be down there for years with your father cutting the turf and then you'd be looking forward to the break after four or five hours of sodding the turf, cutting it and stacking it. Finally, you'd sit down and have your tea and your biscuits and your homemade bread – there was nothing as nice. You wouldn't get as good in a restaurant.

Tea is also a great pick-me-up on the building sites. I'm on building sites fifty years, since I was about thirteen years of age, and tea is terrible important. At one time on the building sites the old builders always had a 'tea boy'. The tea boy would start off that way to serve his time. He was used for two things: to make the tea and to run to the shop to get the cigarettes or a newspaper for the lads but his official title was 'tea boy'. Especially on the school holidays, all the young lads were on the sites and there was no Health and Safety that time. At the weekend all the contractors and builders on the site would throw him a few bob so it often turned out that he was nearly getting better paid than the builders. No site that time went without a tea boy because instead of having the grown-ups wasting time going to the shop, the tea boy ran to the shop, and instead of having the adults making the tea in the billycans the young lad would have the tea made. That was in the 1960s until the late 1970s before all the new Health and Safety

On the building site (l–r): Tom McDonald, George Browne, George Browne Snr and Ruaan Labuschagne.

regulations put an end to the tea boys. In actual fact, a lot of the tea boys went on to become big builders. If he was a good tea boy, the contractors on the site would say 'that's a good young lad, I'll give him an apprenticeship'. That's how a lot of lads started.

I always bring tea on holidays. If you go to Spain or other countries you'd always bring your teabags because you can't beat Barry's tea and you'd always bring Jacob's biscuits and things like that. In a lot of countries the tea isn't as good quality. The water is not the same and that makes a hell of a difference. The missus would put the tea into the suitcase and more than likely the Mikado biscuits that you couldn't get out there.

Before the teabags, we used tea leaves. I remember an aunty from England and she'd boil the water, warm the pot first, throw it out and then put in your two scoops, then brew it and you daren't go near that pot until the tea had brewed, and it'd be strained out with a strainer. Then the teabags came in. The great thing about the loose tea was there was a terrible lot of old people going around telling the fortune, reading the tea leaves – the teabags did away with that. My granny used to read the cups. I remember being in my granny's and people would have a cup of tea and she'd turn it upside down on the saucer and before they left she'd read their cup. It was a very serious thing at the time – people really believed it.

Years ago, one of my mates went on a tour across Europe, Frank Murphy and the wife, but they brought back teabags from Denmark, or somewhere, because there were no teabags at the time in Ireland. So Frank brought the teabags back as a present for his mother. The next time he visited her, says she 'Frank, do you know something, them tea leaves are terrible small'. She didn't know what the teabags were for, so she was after getting a scissors and cut all the teabags and poured it into a tea caddy.

In 1950, Dublin Zoo introduced the Chimpanzee Tea Party that was to become a popular
event for many years at the zoo. Four young chimpanzees were chosen to have tea on the
lawn near the monkey house, and visitors would sit in a wide circle around them. They were
sometimes dressed in big nappies, bonnets, dresses or dungarees. Children loved to see the
young chimps throwing food and turning over their mugs, behaviour discouraged in young
children. COURTESY DUBLIN ZOO

MARY McEVOY

Mary McEvoy is one of Ireland's best-loved actresses, who played Biddy in RTÉ soap *Glenroe*, from 1983 to 2000. She also appeared on stage in *Big Maggie*, *Sive*, *The Field*, *The Vagina Monologues*, *Shirley Valentine* and *Dancing at Lughnasa*. She is a regular panellist on TV3's show *Midday* and a radio contributor on Newstalk.

Tea is love. It seems to be the touchstone of everything, a substitute for love, embarrassment, nurturing, but actually quite a good substitute because people understand the language of it. As an actor when I arrive at a new venue, if I need grounding, a cup of tea really helps. While a cup of coffee would be my pre-show drink to give me a bit of pep for the show, a cup of tea is what you need when you first arrive.

I wouldn't be a massive tea drinker but I do associate tea with comfort. I remember being in an accident a couple of years ago; thankfully nobody was hurt, but we were all in shock, and everybody was running around with cups of tea and sugar. There's just something about making someone a cup of tea that means much more than the actual action which is simply giving someone a drink. A glass of water just wouldn't have the same effect.

It's almost like a spell. In our modern society we don't have many rituals any more, whereas in ancient times we had so many rituals, and there were so many rules of hospitality. Now the only welcoming ritual we have is to make a cup of tea for someone.

Tea has become so ingrained in Irish society, you would think it had been in Ireland since before St Patrick. It really is a social oil here, and it isn't going out of fashion. The panini and ciabatta generation still love a cup of tea. We've hung onto that, it's one of the few things that haven't changed in this country.

When I go to France and visit friends, people don't give you anything when you arrive, they just sit there, and you think 'I want something in my hand'. You want to be offered a cup of tea, or it seems cold and unanchored. You don't feel as welcome. And of course, you might not want it, but it's the ritual of it. It's a kind of language and has a grounding influence and coffee doesn't have the same effect at all.

I don't have a favourite cup but I do have cups I go back to all the time. I had an old cup that I used to always use until it was broken, and my mother loved it, and of course that was about my connection with her. There are certain cups I will always wash for tea. There are also cups I'll have coffee in that I won't have tea in. I have a big mug that was given to me by a friend and that's my coffee mug. I won't have anything except coffee in that mug. But I'd always drink tea from a cup. I don't even use the saucer, but I have a cup that is lovely – porcelain. I think the shape of cups is quite important – the rounder cup is better. I don't like the ones that go straight out, and the inside has to be a light colour so you can judge the intensity of the tea. The more I think about it, we have an awful lot of self-imposed rules!

The quotient of milk is very important. I don't like weak tea: I like a strong tea but I like the thickness of the milk in it, I don't like a thin tea. You need full milk for a good cup of tea.

My mother used to always make me use the teabag twice. It wasn't meanness – she just hated waste – but there is something about putting the cold teabag into your cup that's off-putting.

In Paris, there is a tea shop chain called Mariage Frères, and it's extraordinary to go in and see the endless varieties of tea and yet you still find yourself looking for your ordinary breakfast tea. They have every blend of tea known to man, and you still go back to plain old Irish tea. I think after the madness of the Celtic Tiger years, we are embracing the simple things. You see even the most truly sophisticated people enjoying their good old mug of farmer's tea.

It's quite hard to get a nice cup of tea. The tea you are served in hotels can be awful. You order a pot of tea and you get one teabag in this stainless steel teapot. It's an insult. One little teabag floating around and none of the lids fits properly, so they spill. No, no, no, you have to have it right.

I wouldn't bring teabags abroad because I drink coffee abroad. But my mother always brought teabags when we travelled together, and we used to bring sandwiches for the plane. This was before you had to buy everything on board. Some people even brought the rashers and sausages.

I abhor and hate herbal tea, or as I call it 'horrible tea'. The only one that is nice is rooibos tea, from South Africa because you can put milk in it, so it's like a proper tea.

While working on 'Glenroe', I can only imagine how many cups of tea I made as Biddy.

While working on *Glenroe*, I can only imagine how many cups of tea I made in character, as Biddy. Life for those characters literally revolved around cups of tea. It's extraordinary really, and there was never any coffee on set. When the writers put two or three people together in one place to discuss something enormously life-shattering, it usually took place around a pot of tea at a table. Even the furniture referred to tea. There were about ninety-seven cups hanging on the dresser in the kitchen and only two cups were used. Tea was so much a part of everything in Irish society that even in the *Glenroe* life, you had to start thinking about it. It was just there all the time. That's what you were doing if you were doing a scene in the kitchen, nothing else but making tea.

I remember years ago, on a trip to Japan, we witnessed the tea ceremony, which is amazing. I thought that ritual could never happen in Ireland, but once, a group of Buddhists and I, for a laugh, put on an Irish tea ceremony where everyone was lorrying spoons of sugar and milk into their mugs, and stirring it around and when it was finished the lads all poured it into their saucers and slurped it. That was our Irish tea ceremony.

After a funeral when you go back to your house, suddenly these fairies have appeared from nowhere, i.e. your neighbours, and magically everything is taken care of, and the Burcos are going, and there are big teapots everywhere. Again there's that language of tea, the comfort of it. Someone making you sit down and handing you a cup of tea involves so much more than the simple gesture that it is. There's just wonderful comfort in it. When I go to a wake, it is a lovely thing to see everyone sitting around with the person who has passed away. You can say goodbye to them personally, and you're chatting and you're having tea and you're handing around the apple tart. It's a lovely passing from one life to another, and if there's any essence of that person left, how lovely it must be. Of course, you also have hot, sweet tea for shock. Nobody knows why, but it works. I could just imagine if the Minister for Health decided to ban tea, I'd say antidepressants and Valium sales would go through the roof because tea provides so much therapy.

ANDREA DUFFY

Andrea Duffy teaches Junior and Senior Infants at Scoil Colmcille, Glengad, on the Inishowen Peninsula, County Donegal.

In Donegal, tea is always called 'tae'. The broader the accent the better. Everybody says 'tae' here.

A friend of mine, who used to work in Letterkenny Hospital, was clearing out the psychiatric unit there and came across old records for one woman who was committed for excessive tea drinking, way back in the early 1900s. But I could see why that would happen because I drink a lot of tea and by evening it has its effects and I could see how someone might think you were mad.

One woman was committed for excessive tea drinking, way back in the early 1900s

It depends whether you are caffeine sensitive or not. I drink just one cup of coffee a day – if I drink two I go wild hyper and then I get the shakes, and then I go low. Everyone's different. I drink decaf when I'm pregnant. My husband Paul says I'm a far nicer person when I'm on decaf – I'm calmer.

Everybody I know has a specific type of tea. I like it so strong you could walk on it and I leave the teabag in for two or three minutes and the tea should look nice and black in the mug. I don't take milk. I got onto the black tea in Lough Derg on the pilgrimage. I went to Lough Derg six different times between the ages of twenty-five and thirty-five. I'm not a wildly religious person but I cannot wait to go back since I had children because it will be three days of complete peace: there's no phone, no TV, no newspapers, no radio, there's complete silence. You could be meditating, or doing anything; you're just in there paddling. Everyone hates the black tea there but I think it's no bother. There's no milk because it's not a penance if you don't go without the milk. You see people shovelling in sugar instead of milk.

I'm from Malin Head, on the Inishowen Peninsula, but I have been around the world. I drank tea in China. Anywhere I go, I always bring my tea with me. I remember once being caught in Morocco without my tea. I don't drink alcohol and my husband would come and sit on the balcony and have his glass of wine at night but I always wanted my cup of tea. So not being able to have my cup of tea on the balcony in the evening ruined the holiday. My number one priority is the teabags in the case.

Sometimes I have visitors who don't drink tea and I find it so unsociable. They probably think they're doing you a favour, but I'm sitting there not knowing what to do with my hands. You're preparing the tea while you're talking and then you're drinking your tea or you're eating a biscuit. And if somebody hasn't had a cup of tea, you feel like you've been a terrible host and you just don't think they have had a good visit.

There's also etiquette involved. It's very important to know how long to leave them sitting there before you offer the cup of tea. You don't just let them in the door and say, 'right, do you want a cup of tea?' You have a wee chit-chat first and then make the tea and somebody has to be in the room with them while you're preparing the tea. You must know when to offer a second cup and if you leave it too late, they get up and go.

Presentation is important, too, although it depends on the visitor. If your friend is coming in, a mug is fine, but I think if your mother-in-law is coming in, it's nice to be able to pull out even just a wee bit of Denby. I notice when I teach Junior Infants, if you do matching exercises, they don't know that 'cup' and 'saucer' go together. They don't even know 'milk jug'.

(L–r): Teachers Denise Doherty, Olivia Kelly, Mary Harkin, Andrea Duffy and Elaine Byrne enjoying a tea break in the staffroom at Scoil Colmcille, Glengad, County Donegal.

There are places where you would take tea and places you wouldn't if the tea is bad. It's just that people make tea differently. If I make tea for my sisters, because I drink strong tea, there's many a time I have handed it to them and they dump it down the sink and make it themselves. They just dip a teabag in their mug – they just waste teabags. An aunt of mine likes half a cup of milk, half tea. And you can't have your tea without your biscuits. You can have coffee without biscuits but not tea: tea always has to have an accompaniment.

My best ever cup of tea was when I came back to work after my maternity leave. Because I also had a toddler at home, every time you sat down for a cup of tea they'd be climbing over you or they want something or you're afraid you would scald them, so there was no point. But coming back to work and having a designated time for tea, you actually sit down to have your cup of tea and a biscuit: that was pure pleasure. Tea breaks are lovely in our staff room. If the kettle's not boiled, you are all standing around not knowing what to do. Nobody relaxes until they are sitting with a cup of tea. I think it is a comfort and the colder the weather the more cups of tea you'll down. Whoever goes into the staffroom first makes a pot of tea.

You could say everything is solved with a cup of tea. I'm the sort who needs to be up and running around but it makes you sit down. Life without tea would be dreadful. Tea does two things: it's a contradiction, but it both comforts and invigorates you.

JOHN, ORLA & NIAMH TRANT

John, Orla and Niamh Trant are seventeen-year-old triplets and sixth-year students from Newcastle, County Dublin.

JOHN TRANT

I started drinking tea properly about three years ago. Before that it was just every now and again. It was to be sociable, when I was working. I work on a farm up the road from our own farm, on weekends and holidays. I help out with everything on the farm: milking, spreading slurry, whatever needs to be done. It's great. I want to work on our family farm when I finish school. The others would go in for a cup of tea and I would be just sitting there with nothing. They were always offering me a cup of tea, and I would always say 'no'. Eventually I thought I'd better start. It was almost peer pressure.

I also did a job fitting blinds as well as the farming and you were in people's houses, and they always offer you a cup of tea so it's a good time to talk business and it's good for business. Because that customer will tell a friend 'he fitted blinds for me, he's a nice man'.

I drink tea with milk and two sugars. I used to have it without sugar when I started, but I found it hard to drink so I added sugar, and I liked it then.

My favourite brand is Barry's tea. My mother is a big tea drinker and she'd always bring Barry's on holidays with us. She and my dad drank tea from beakers when they were babies – they love tea. If my mother doesn't have tea in the mornings she gets a headache. She actually didn't want any of her kids to drink tea – to start the habit. She thought it was bad for our teeth. But we used to sneak down to our nana's for a cup of tea.

I do have a favourite mug – it's just a big mug with a big heavy handle. I've got chubby fingers. When I'm working I'd drink about five cups of tea. If we're working out in the fields all day, we bring a flask out with us and have tea and sandwiches outside.

Irish people are obsessed with tea.

ORLA TRANT

Tea is a very big thing for me. But my eldest brother and sister don't drink tea and the rest of us do, so there is a rift forming. We're a dying breed.

After dinner my mam and I always have tea, but my Dad doesn't. It was a tradition in my Dad's family that they always had tea at three o'clock, so he still does that, while we have it after dinner. I get really insulted if my mam doesn't make me a cup of tea after dinner. It actually happened yesterday. She came into the sitting room with a cup of tea. I was lying on the sofa looking forward to my tea. I said, 'Mam, come on, where's my tea?' I was really upset actually. She forgot me. I even put the kettle on.

And you always have to have teabags at parties. Niamh, John and I had a big party at the start of the midterm break so you had to go and look for things to bring to the house, finger food and whatever, and a lot of teabags and extra milk in case you run out. Tea is very important for the after party. At our age, if you don't drink tea you get a big slagging, 'what's he like, he doesn't drink tea!'

Of course we started drinking tea in my nana's house. My nana had three mugs for us in her house, one that says Niamh, one Orla and one that says John.

Or when you come in after a night out the first thing you do is put on the kettle for tea. It might be five o'clock in the morning – like, if I come home from babysitting at five o'clock, I always have to have a cup of tea before I go to bed. It's just something: when you come home, you have to have tea.

I think the water is important to the taste of your tea too. In my friend Laura's house, her water and the tea tastes different. She lives in Citywest and I'm in Newcastle.

We always bring teabags abroad too. It's a communal thing, a little cup of home. Tea is a very social thing. When you go to someone's house and they offer you tea and you say no, it's almost insulting. It's nice to say yes, and sit down over a cup of tea and have a chat. I met my boyfriend's mam and dad for the first time the other day. I was going in the door and I was a bit nervous and apprehensive, so when his mam said 'would you like a cup of tea?' I said 'yes', straight away. It's an ice-breaker. And a few times later, I was in his house and I thought to myself 'I think it's time' and I went over and I put on the kettle and made my own cup of tea. That's when you know things are serious!

NIAMH TRANT

I started drinking tea down in my nana's house, I wasn't allowed drink it at home because my mam was afraid it was bad for our teeth. So I used to go down to my nana's and probably caused more problems for my teeth. She'd give us a small cup of tea with three big spoons of sugar in it and a load of milk. We were only about five. Nana never saw the harm in a cup of tea.

I'm a triplet, and when Mam left the house the three of us would sneak tea. And when we were in trouble and we were sent to our room, we used to climb out the window and our nana lived next door so we would go down and have a cup of tea with her. I'd say my mam knew. But I remember when we went to the dentist she'd say 'Do you drink tea?' and we would say no.

Tea is definitely an ice-breaker between people. If you go to someone's house or there's a different mix of people, especially with teenagers, and you go 'does anyone want a cup of tea?' you then say 'how would you like your tea?' and you can have a bit of craic talking about it, because everyone likes it differently. I think there's trust involved in making someone's tea as well, because I hate making tea for someone I don't know – I'm afraid I'll get it wrong because there are so many different ways of taking it. So I often say to people, I don't trust you enough with my tea, I don't know you well enough!

I'm very fussy. I like it really strong. You have to get the sugar right too, I like a big teaspoon of sugar, but not too big, and just a drop of milk. It's the same way my dad takes it actually. So I always get him or my sister Orla to make my tea. I don't let my brother John make my tea – he gets it wrong every time. Orla gets it right.

When someone comes to your house and you offer them a cup of tea and they say 'no', what do you say? You don't know what to do. Give them milk?

It has to be Barry's. Lyons isn't the same. You'll know if it's Lyons or some cheap tea. It's like, 'do you not care about your cup of tea?' You have to care about your tea.

I used to drink about five cups a day, but I had to cut back. I was going to bed all hyper. Even last night I had a cup of tea before bed just to chill out and I didn't get to sleep until around three o'clock. It makes me talk in my sleep as well. My sister Orla and I share a room and she sleeps above me in the bunk bed and every time I drink tea going to bed, she hears me talking. I'd be afraid of what I'd be saying.

Nana always gets me to make her tea now. She doesn't like anyone else making it when we come down. She says 'are you making the tea?' and I say 'no, you're making it'. She just sits there and laughs as if I'm joking. And waits for me to make the tea. Or she just waits until I ask her does she want tea and then she says 'only if you're making one.' She tries to guilt-trip me into it. She's gas.

I have a favourite mug, with Podge and Rodge on it. The mug is very important – it's really thin around the edge. The worst bit about tea is when your biscuit falls into it. You have to dunk your biscuit!

The worst bit about tea is when your biscuit falls into it.

Two old ladies from Marlborough Street whose house caught fire being offered a cup of tea by their neighbours, 1960s. COURTESY INDEPENDENT NEWSPAPERS IRELAND

BRIAN KENNY

Brian Kenny runs the Outdoor Swimming Ireland Website and has been known to swim for longer than three minutes.

www.outdoorswimming.ie

COURTESY LEONIE O'DOWD

COLD WATER HOT TEA

February is the cruellest month. It's meant to be spring but it most definitely is not. The milder weather of April and May might be on the horizon but right now the water is bloody freezing.

Stick to the tried-and-tested routine. Get changed quickly and repeat: 'This will be over in approximately four minutes.' Stride quickly to the water and don't think. Plunge in and swim fast before the icy water knows you're there. Quick strokes, deep gasps. Don't think of the cold, don't think of the numbness. Think, instead, of the shiny flask waiting for you in a few minutes' time.

Nearly there. A few more strokes and the mandatory three minutes are up (all right, maybe two minutes, thirty seconds). Struggle out of the water, looking cool and unconcerned. Remember the golden rule of winter swimming: never, ever admit that the water froze the goolies off you. Certain phrases are acceptable: 'not as bad as yesterday', 'that's a fresh one', 'grand once you get in'. If you ever say 'Jaysus, that was absolutely freezing', you face instant scorn and automatic excommunication.

Head quickly to towel and clothes. The small lady next to me must be over seventy, about five foot nothing, and no more than six stone. She arrived on her bike. 'So you just had a quick in and out,' she remarks. Bloody cheek, I was in for at least three minutes. Ignore this monstrous slight. A quick dry and paradise awaits.

Wrapped in coat and hat, reach for the flask and pour the hot, black tea. Add the sugar. No milk – milk is for wimps. The hot liquid warms body and soul, reaching to the frozen toes and the throbbing fingers. Hands wrapped around my cup, I hold on for dear life as the tea restores me.

I look out to sea and my seventy-year-old friend is casually swimming up and down. I'm surprised she's not on her back, sunbathing. But she's wearing those swimming gloves and shoes. Sure, anybody could to that. I lean back and pour myself another cup. With the tea warming me all over and the blood flowing through my veins, I make an important decision – I'm never going to wear those things when I'm seventy.

JOAN FREEMAN

In 2003, Joan Freeman, a practising psychologist, closed down her counselling business to dedicate her time to helping people who were suicidal. After three years of research, she opened up Pieta House, the centre for the prevention of self-harm and suicide, in Lucan, County Dublin. It quickly became a respected and recognised service for those who are suicidal. Pieta now have two outreach centres in Tallaght and Finglas, as well as two centres of excellence in Ballyfermot and Limerick. In 2012, more than 3,000 people came to Pieta House for help and the numbers contacting the service are rising all the time.

COURTESY SASKO LAZAROV/PHOTOCALL IRELAND

The cup of tea here in Pieta House is absolutely crucial. People who come here aren't given a choice – the minute they come in, they are given their tray, with a little pot of tea and some biscuits. I suppose that comes from my upbringing. People were always offered tea when they arrived at my mother's house, it was so important to welcome the visitor to your home.

I come from a family of eight, so of course there was never a biscuit in the house, ever, and in the unlikely event of us buying a packet, as soon as the visitors went, we were like savages and would eat everything. My parents couldn't afford biscuits, but what they could afford was toast, so again, whether people liked it or not, they were given tea and toast when they came in. This was a ritual that was really important: it was the most welcoming thing my mother could do, but there was also something very comforting about it.

I remember very clearly my very first cup of tea, when I was about four or five years of age. It's funny that when I had my own children, there was no way I was going to give my children tea or coffee. But in those days you did – it was a hot drink with about three or four spoons of sugar in it. I remember coming back from Mass, and all eight of us were standing around in the kitchen, which was tiny, and I remember standing there, drinking a cup of tea and thinking it was the most delicious thing. There's definitely a comfort with tea. So I transferred that nurturing, that welcoming cup of tea to Pieta House when we started. Tea actually has such an important role here. There are three things that are ingrained in Pieta House, which can never be changed. One is that the person is greeted by name and brought into the reception room; the second is that they are given their tray with their tea, and the third is that they are offered a seat on a couch, and the assessor sits on a footstool about eighteen inches from them – to engage with them and listen. So again we're immediately serving them – we're serving them with a cup of tea and we're serving them with our help.

That approach comes from two sources – it comes from my home and upbringing, and secondly if it was my child or loved one who was in trouble, this is how I would want them to be treated, it's as simple as that.

We have volunteers here all the time making tea for people and for their families

It is so important we have volunteers here all the time making tea for people and for their families. We're not a drop-in centre: we work by appointments, so that we can ensure there is a therapist available for the hour for that client. But sometimes people drop in when they are very distressed. I think one of my most vivid memories of a cup of tea here at Pieta House is from one such day. We were only open about a year, and I was up at the top of the house and Avril, the Centre Manager, came up to me and said, 'Joan, there's a lady downstairs and she's quite distressed; is there any way you could just talk to her and we will make an appointment for her?' I said yes, so I came down, and when I walked into the room I found this woman sitting at the edge of the couch, hunched forward, with a towel around her shoulders – it had been lashing rain all evening – and the towel was over her head and around her shoulders and she was holding a mug of tea, and there was a two-bar electric fire beaming at her and I said to myself, 'that is pure minding and pure nurturing' – the cup of tea and being dried off and knowing that it's all right and being welcomed by people who wanted to help. When I saw that, I thought this is so right. I will always remember that lady sitting there, being comforted, as long as I live.

I do love tea. Most nights I bring a mug of tea up to bed. I might drink only half of it but again the thought of having a cup of tea, snuggled in bed – again it's all to do with comfort and nurturing. But it's only now I realise what a feature tea has been in my life.

Some people have such ritual around tea. My sister only uses tea leaves, but I tease her that she thinks of herself as a little bit posh. But I do remember, when we were small, turning up the cups to try and read our fortune from the tea leaves. As if we could tell, for heaven's sake.

I was born in Dublin and then we lived in England for a while. When we moved back, I couldn't get over the fact that Irish people drink tea with their meal, whereas we didn't, we had tea long after a meal. I remember being shocked that Irish people often drink tea while eating their dinner.

I don't take milk or sugar in my tea – I gave up sugar as a child during Lent, and later I gave up milk again during Lent or for a diet or something – but I couldn't stand tea with milk in it now, I'd absolutely hate it. Do I have a favourite mug? It has to be the biggest mug I can get.

PATRICK McDONNELL

Patrick McDonnell is a stand-up comedian, actor and writer. He has appeared in several award winning shows such as *Moone Boy, Stew, Naked Camera* and *The Savage Eye*, but is best remembered as tea- and cake-loving monster Eoin McLove in *Father Ted*.

COURTESY DAVID McDONNELL

I take my tea relatively strong with a dash of milk. A 'dash' to me means a mere splash and nothing more. I wish someone would properly standardise milk measurements: the scale could go from 'black' up to a 'dash', a 'small sup', a 'sup', a 'good sup', all the way to 'plenty'. As it is, measurements are entirely subjective and blatantly open to abuse. One should always be allowed to add the milk oneself. Only occasionally does someone else get it right. It's presumptuous and disrespectful of personal boundaries to add milk to someone else's tea. It's a slippery slope to murder. You are ultimately disempowering the other person. I despise myself when I just smile and accept a cup that's basically just hot milk when I've said that I just take a dash of milk. If I were a stronger person I might insist on putting it in myself.

I can't stand sugar either. Sugary tea tastes like poison to me. It completely drowns out the subtle flavours. It's curious how two people might say that they both enjoy tea but in reality enjoy a completely different experience. One may like it sugary and milky, while someone else, such as myself, may prefer it the correct way, that is, with just a dash of milk in a mug.

It's nice to sip tea from a china cup now and again, and I would have to say it possibly does enhance the sensual experience to do so, but I could never sip from china first thing in the morning. That would be wrong. It's okay with cake in the afternoon but not with sausages in the morning.

I'd say I drink about four mugs per day, but if I have to write or concentrate on anything in particular that would generally go up to about seven.

I could never drink black tea in public for fear of giving the impression that I was some sort of self-denying, hard-core Catholic.

Why do Irish people love tea so much? It has everything to do with our colonial past. Most western societies prefer coffee but, because of our absorption/coercion into the British Empire, we prefer tea. When they sold their tatty cotton goods to their new colonies they couldn't come all the way back with an empty ship – they needed to bring home commodities to force down the necks of their defeated subjects, the balance of trade and all that. We were relatively selective in what we retained from our subjugated years but tea is probably the best one. It made a cold meal hot and it perked us up sufficiently to slave in the fields we'd just lost possession of.

I drink Lyons Gold Blend. The original Green Blend just doesn't do it for me. Barry's was never consumed in my house for the obvious political reasons. Typhoo and Twinings were too British.

I have two favourite mugs. My kids bought me a 'Daddy Cool' mug in the past few years, but it's the wrong shape: a mug needs to be cylindrical and in no way conical, otherwise it loses its heat too quickly. Privately my favourite is a 'Late Show with David Letterman' mug a friend got me in New York a few years back.

I hated tea when I was a kid. I grew up in the era before the teabag became popular in Ireland so all we had was loose tea and I hated finding bits of leaf and twig floating about on the surface. My mother had the little sieves somewhere but I don't think we ever used them.

All tea was made in a pot and the further down your share came determined how many bits you got. I didn't try it again until I was in college and it was when I found that I didn't have to put sugar in and could modify the milk that I got a taste for it. On the rare occasions I studied, I felt that hot beverages helped me to concentrate. Coffee made me jittery and slightly aggressive so I stuck to a calming brew.

Tea has come into its own when I have been the recipient of bad news. It is incredibly comforting when I've had a shock or been told of a death. I often wonder what people did before the introduction of tea to this country. I'm sure the British knew what they were doing when they conquered us: 'We'll have all your land, thanks, but here's a nice cup of tea to cheer you up.'

> *Tea has come into its own when I have been the recipient of bad news*

In the *Father Ted* episode 'The night of the nearly dead', Mrs Doyle won a competition to have tea and cake with the character I portrayed, Eoin McLove. I therefore had the pleasure of having tea with perhaps its most famous Irish proponent. I don't think she said 'go on, go on' to me but it was a thrill nonetheless. The real Eoin McLove famously has mass tea rallies in Donegal with his post-menopausal army. I wouldn't say anyone messes with his tea; I'd say he could literally have you killed if you put the wrong amount of milk or sugar in his cup.

Patrick McDonnell (right) playing tea lover Eoin McLove, with Dermot Morgan in *Fr Ted*.
COURTESY HAT TRICK PRODUCTIONS LTD.

PAT LYSAGHT

Pat Lysaght, from Naas, County Kildare, is a Technician in RTÉ's television department.

I drink about ten cups of tea a day. I like my mug to have a white interior so you can see the texture of the tea.

At work you have to carry the tea a long way from the canteen and you can't work with a mug that's not sealed, what with all the equipment we use. But I don't like those travel mugs – the taste of tea from them is just not what it should be and they're badly designed because they're narrower at the bottom so they fall over too easily. I really wanted to be able to use a delph mug. Getting a decent cup of tea is so important to me so I said to myself, 'you can't buy a delph one with a cap on it so what will I do?' I took the cap off a travel mug and went to the shops and had the cap in my pocket and eventually through trial and error I found a delph mug that would fit it. Now I have a delph mug with a cap – it's brilliant!

Getting a decent cup of tea is so important to me

MARK ORFORD

Mark Orford is a freelance radio researcher and producer who works in and around Dublin on an all-too-irregular basis.

COURTESY CLARE McQUAID

Tea for me is a new thing. Unlike many people in Ireland I'm a relative newcomer to the wonders of tea, as I started drinking it only about three years ago. Many more seasoned tea drinkers may scoff at my lack of experience but because I've only started out on my tea journey, my memories of falling deeply in love with this brown liquid are vivid, lucid and immediate – in fact, I'm still falling in love.

My first memories of tea aren't good. I thought it smelled very strange, and the odd time my parents would try and foist it on me I would have a little sip, swallow it down and make a loud groan of disgust, along with an audible '*ewwww*'. I quickly decided at the age of about nine that tea was not for me.

So what happened to make me change? To be perfectly honest, I flirted with the idea of becoming a fully fledged tea drinker when I met

I flirted with the idea of becoming a fully fledged tea drinker when I met my girlfriend

my girlfriend, and would have the odd cup here and there if only to stop the coldness of staying in her cold flat on Baggot St. But there was one single cup that changed the way I felt about tea. As I grew into my twenties I began to get more hungover than I ever was during my early childhood. I was going to Belfast with a pal and when I called to his house, he offered me a rasher sandwich and a cup of tea. He told me that this combination would not only set me up for the car journey to Belfast but it would also fix my hangover. Miraculously this combination worked a treat, and off we drove. And from then on I knew it was tea for me.

These days I would usually have about two to three cups a day maximum. The process is to make sure that I have a certain amount of time set aside in order to make myself a perfect cup of tea every time. Ideally, I'll leave the teabag to soak for as long as possible, while I do some household chores – really quick ones like making sure the radiator is on as high as it can go (that's a chore, isn't it?) so my cup of tea can be enjoyed at its optimum level. Then I'll return to my cup (it's a Super Furry Animals one) and squeeze the teabag on the side of the cup with the spoon, to get some extra strength out of the bag. I'll then put a tiny drop of milk in it. I like my tea strong: my tea-making mantra is 'strong tea – strong mind'.

It's worth noting that I still find it odd to see children or teenagers actively drinking tea. I don't know why, but I'm almost sure that this is a fully normal thing to think.

I'm not 100 per cent sure why it is that Irish people go mad for tea. My best guess is that it's something to do with our soggy climate, and our hereditary instinct means that we've picked the best drink to help us get through life on a particularly damp and windy island on the edge of Europe. And what a wonderful drink it is. I can't (and don't want to) imagine what they drink on tropical islands – probably something really boring like water.

DENYSE WOODS

Denyse Woods, who also writes as Denyse Devlin, is the author of five novels and the Artistic Director of the West Cork Literary Festival.
COURTESY TAMZIN MERIVALE

CAMELLIA SINENSIS

Imagine my surprise. 'SCALD THE POT' read a sign by the water geyser in a garden centre café outside Cork. It was frankly shocking to see tea taken so seriously, and another sign confirmed that this establishment was run by someone who actually cared. It read: 'Making Tea is an Art.' Alleluia to that! Warming the pot can make the difference between good tea and the vile brew we're usually served, and the brew is usually vile because few people in the hospitality industry appear to have the slightest inkling that tea making is, indeed, an art, and this in spite of the fact that the Irish are amongst the biggest tea drinkers in the world. So does it follow that we are discerning tea drinkers, or any good at making it? On the basis of what passes for tea in most outlets, the evidence suggests the contrary.

According to most figures, Ireland is the No. 1 per capita consumer of tea in the world, with an annual consumption of 2.71kg per person. This figure might surprise anyone who has travelled to an Arab country, for example, where you can't walk ten paces without being offered a sublime glass of tea. But here's the thing about the biggest per capita tea consumers on the planet: most of us only drink tea at home. Out and about, we tend to order coffee, in part because it is considered better value – across the board, people seem to agree that, in most places, a teabag let loose in some hot water comes vastly overpriced. However, a straw poll of my email contacts yielded an even stronger case for coffee over tea – outside the home, tea is too often undrinkable. There seems to be no disagreement that in cafés, hotels and bars, coffee is the safer bet. In keeping with the worldwide trend, baristas have become de rigueur in Irish establishments: staff are not only specially trained to make good coffee, but are expected to practise, perfect, and even reveal their inner selves through latte art. And while these shamrocks, tulips and rosettes are absorbing the concentration of their froth-pouring creators, the most recent addition to the staff, and therefore the least experienced, is chucking a teabag into a pot. After all, anyone can pour hot water over a teabag, right? To add insult to injury, the tea drinker then has to sit and watch while their coffee companion is offered refill after refill, and all for the price of one cup. No such generosity for tea drinkers – after all, they can get several cups from the one pot, right? Absolutely. If you squeeze the teabag, and then squeeze the one-person pot, you might just produce another half-cup of stewed tea.

'The worst tea,' a friend writes, 'is when they bring you the hot water in a cup with the fancy teabag on a plate. People don't understand that tea needs to brew.' This type of service – the bare teabag on a plate – is a poor attempt to create some kind of flourish, and totally misses the whole point of tea: that it is patient, that it likes to sit and think before revealing itself at its very best. This presentation is also humiliating, since now we even have to dunk the damn teabag ourselves, lift it out (even though the tag has probably fallen into the scalding water), stop it swinging and dribbling everywhere, and somehow squeeze the water out of the flailing bag without burning our fingers, while our coffee companions are luxuriously slurping their spoon around the latte art, creating swirls and furls where, moments ago, had been a mocha heart. The coffee-drinking experience is one of care and elegance, but there is nothing so ugly as a used teabag drooping over the side of a saucer, the cup sitting in its drippings.

There used to be ceremony about tea in Ireland. There were dedicated tea rooms, where tea was served in china pots and china cups (for good reason: china retains heat), and such places still exist around the world, even in coffee-crazed countries like France and Italy, where patrons often have to queue for a table. In Ireland, with rare exceptions, tea drinkers are consumer scum on the floor of the hospitality industry. Those popular tin teapots might be hardy, but they make tea taste of, well, tin, and tea served in big wide coffee cups quickly gets cold. The water has most likely been over-boiled, allowing oxygen to escape, thereby damaging the flavour, or not boiled – another common crime – which makes tea taste like a botanist's mistake. And yet tea drinkers don't complain. We don't complain because most of us are drinking coffee.

Tea drinkers don't ask for much. We don't need cucumber sandwiches and doilies. We don't even need tea leaves; a good teabag is fine. We're not looking for a million zillion different mixes of leaf, perfumed or otherwise. We just want a nice cup, made with a bit of heart, and we'd rather not go to a five-star hotel for the privilege, and take out a mortgage in the process.

* * * *

The warehouse at Barry's Tea smells of Africa. Crates rise in stacks to the ceiling, most having come from Rwanda, Kenya, Uganda – since all Irish blends include a significant component of East African teas – and, of course, India. The tea has come a long way, through a long process. The tea plant spends six months in nurseries and then four years in plantations, where it grows into a three-foot high table, at the top of which the youngest leaves, in pairs (like parents), cradle a new bud; these are the ones that are handpicked by workers, who pick an average of 60kg of green tea per day. They have often been with the same cooperatives, such as the KTDA (Kenyan Tea Development Authority), for generations and their work, in many cases, has allowed them to educate their children – indeed, many of the professional classes in tea-growing countries have tea-picking parents. The picked leaf is then examined and weathered in local factories, where, in long shallow troughs holding about 1,000kg of tea, it is given twelve to sixteen hours to 'wither', while hot air is blown over and under the troughs. It loses 35 per cent of its moisture during withering, and goes on to endure the 'CTT' stage – cut, torn and tear – in huge revolving barrels that cut it into different sizes. Next, in continuous fermentation machines, it turns green, then copper, and finally, after a spell in 'flubed' (fluid bed) dryers, black. Vibro sifter tea machines – huge vibrating machines which have different-sized meshes – grade it into Broken Pekoe (loose-pack tea), Pekoe Fannings and Pekoe Dust (both for teabags). At auctions in Mombasa, Kochi, Siliguri and Guwahati, indigenous brokers bid for their clients, and the tea is finally shipped worldwide, where it lands in the cups of professional tasters, who blend according to colour, strength and flavour, aiming always for consistency, since flavour is affected by weather – hard seasons, and gentle ones. So the little bud, picked off its tabletop, fermented, ripped, withered and shipped, reaches the greatest tea-consuming nation in the world, where it is chucked into a boarding-school pot and slapped in front of a customer.

For such a tea-loving nation, it is sad that the exquisite black Indian and African leaf is treated with such disregard by those in the trade. In true tea-drinking cultures it enjoys more respect; it is given time to brew, so that the water may fully swallow the flavour; it is served in china or glass, to hold the heat, and the preparation is as much of a ritual as is serving it, and drinking it. As it should be. This is the oldest of drinks; the most healing of plants – full of antioxidants, it is good for the body and kind to the soul.

So let's give tea the respect it deserves. Next time you're served a tepid mug of drain-water, think of the journey – of the people who planted and transplanted, who picked, bid, boxed and sipped in order that the Irish might have their beloved cup – and send it back to the barista.

Tea chests being unloaded at the docks for McGrath's Tea, 1940s.

ANN STONE

Ann Stone is a housewife, accomplished dancer and mother of three from County Kildare.

This big teapot was used when the priest came to the house for the Station Masses. We filled that up for all the neighbours who came to the house for Mass and we all sat around and chatted afterwards. I have it about thirty years; I can't even remember where I bought it. It holds about twelve cups of tea and I used about eight spoons of tea leaves. Nowadays with teabags, I'd use about ten teabags. It still gets a lot of use for get-togethers, parties and wakes. I've gotten great use out of that teapot – the number of people who have borrowed it for different occasions is amazing! I've never seen them in shops since, so lots of friends and relatives borrow it.

The tea years ago used to come in a tea chest. The box was lined inside with silver paper, like the paper from a cigarette box. A friend told me they used to use the empty tea chest as a playpen for keeping the child in so they wouldn't ramble around the house. And sometimes musicians used the tea chest to make a bass in a band. They would make a 'tea chest bass' out of it, by putting the handle of a sweeping brush through it with strings attached.

Children used to bring a bottle of tea to school and we used to sit the bottles around the stove to keep them warm until lunchtime. When I was a child, a lot of people drank tea out of a tin mug the Travellers made, called a 'bonger'. The Travellers would come to your door and sell their mugs.

Children used to bring a bottle of tea to school

Men would often drink tea out of a saucer. I can still remember my brother Liam drinking tea out of his saucer, sixty years ago. He'd pour the tea from his cup onto the saucer when he was a child, but everyone did it back then, young and old, from the saucer. I don't really know why, maybe to cool it down.

AISLING BROWNE

Aisling Browne is a life coach and lives with her husband and two sons in County Kildare.

About fifteen years ago, I travelled around the world for a year with a boyfriend, and on the way back we stopped in Fiji, for a holiday. We had been camping in a tent for about six months, on a very tight budget, and we were dying for a bit of luxury, so as a treat to ourselves, we booked into a hotel for three nights. The first thing we noticed was that we were able to stand up getting dressed, unlike in the tent, and the second was that there was a kettle in the room, and it seemed like such a luxury to be able to make tea and coffee. So, the first night of our stay, all we did was repeatedly put on the kettle and make tea and coffee. We kept filling the kettle through the spout, not bothering to open the top. My boyfriend had about ten cups of coffee and I had about five cups of tea and we had a great time. The next morning we decided we were going to have more tea and coffee before we went out sightseeing and I went to fill the kettle but I noticed a bit of a rattle so I decided to open it to have a look and inside the kettle was a little gecko lizard that was completely snow white, almost transparent because it had been boiled so many times. I was horrified.

We went down to reception and complained and all they did was give us a new kettle. Eventually I laughed and laughed that my boyfriend had drunk a lot more 'gecko blend' from that kettle than I had.

I have so many memories of important cups of tea in my life – the vital times where the cup of tea may have softened the pain or saved the day or just made life bearable at the time.

One of the most rewarding and deserving cups of tea has to be the one just after childbirth. While I may have deserved a bottle of champagne, a tonne of painkillers and a shopping spree worth millions for doing what I had just done, the cup of tea actually came close to being

One of the most rewarding and deserving cups of tea has to be the one just after childbirth.

enough. That cup of tea and the toast, when you have stopped being sick and the nurses judge you safe to drink, is like nothing else in this world. It is the revival cup – you were at the brink, thinking you would never come back, and then they give you the tea and you realise it's all behind you and you look at your new baby over your cup of tea and at last you feel safe.

Then there's the tea I have with my best friend. I walk into her house and one of the first things she says is 'I'll stick on the kettle' and I know that there will be soul searching, advice, laughter and sometimes tears, and I will always come away feeling so much better.

Three generations taking tea: Aisling, with her sons, Flynn and Dylan, and her mother, Betty Anne, around Betty Anne's kitchen table.

PETER BRADY

Peter Brady lives in Navan and works with Meath County Council as Environmental Awareness Officer. Peter is married to Sarah and has two children, Ruairi and Eimear.

Left: Peter Brady with his daughter Eimear, aged six. COURTESY LISA CROKER

(L–r): oldest boys Philip and William, carrying the bath; Brid, John and Mary with tins; Tony with bucket, Hugh with two kettles and yours truly at the rear, c. 1968.
COURTESY PETER BRADY

The well beside our house usually went dry during the summer and we had to fetch water from the well 500 metres away, down the fields. All my siblings were tasked with a suitably sized container: Cow & Gate baby food tins, kettles, buckets and the bath. I recently came across these old photographs and memories of times gone by flooded back. I grew up in Castletown-Finea, north Westmeath, on the Cavan/Meath border. One photograph shows us fetching water from a well located two fields away on the farm, which was a major task for us children back yonder. This was a regular occurrence during our warm dry summers when we had no rain from June until mid-September, which of course coincided with our school holidays. I wonder what has happened to our climate since then.

We had to fetch water for washing (dishes and bodies), cooking and, of course, the making of tea. Our family were small-time farmers and had a small country pub/grocery. We actually sold loose tea from a great wooden tea chest. I recall, as an eight-year-old, weighing out ounces of tea for local customers and charging amounts like 2½ pennies or three shillings and sixpence, long before the euro. It seemed like a lot of money back then as people were generally quite poor.

We grew up in the 1960s and 1970s, in pre-machinery times, when most of the farming work was done by hand. I had five brothers, so my Dad had lots of free labour available when it came to chores such as turf cutting, hay making, potato planting and harvesting, and so on. The staple diet of the time, for my family at least, was potatoes, bread, milk and tea. I can still recall the refreshing taste of tea during those times of heavy work. One would imagine tea is a particularly welcome refreshment during frosty October days when potatoes were harvested but for some reason, my abiding memory of tea is from hot summer days (and I mean really hot: up to 26 °C) in the hayfield, as we worked at 'turning' or 'rowing' or 'lumping' or 'cocking' hay from early morning. When lunchtime came around at one or two o'clock, it was much needed.

My abiding memory of tea is from hot summer days in the hayfield

My three younger sisters would be tasked with carrying the lunch from the house to the hayfields, sometimes to rented lands five or six miles away, with a bicycle as the only means of transport. The tea would not stay hot for long and my Dad was a stickler for tea, so to ensure the tea retained its true value, my mum duly enveloped the tea – stored in large whiskey bottles – in warm winter socks, the best thermal design of the day. I can still taste that warm, sweet tea gurgling down my throat. After the short rest, chunky sandwiches and a generous helping of sugar-laden hot tea, the human machine was all geared up for the afternoon shift.

When I mention Dad, may he rest in peace, I have to say that he loved his tea and loved it hot. One of his embarrassing habits which I frequently recall was his method of cooling down his tea. He was never one to use much milk and in order to make the tea cool enough to drink: he would pour some onto his saucer, slurp some from the saucer and then pour the remainder back into his cup to cool the tea. This practice was barely acceptable at home with just his family as audience but when I witnessed him do this at the local cattle marts, pubs and the very infrequent family gatherings in some local hostelry, it was quite mortifying.

Happier occasions where tea was central was at the family picnics where the tablecloth was brought out to the local field and our evening tea or picnic was enjoyed in the open air with not a cloud in the sky.

An open-air picnic in the meadow, c. 1970. Clockwise from left: Tony, Philip, Peter, Bríd, William, Hugh, John and Mary Brady. COURTESY PETER BRADY

YVONNE ROSS

Yvonne Ross is a Kilkenny-based goldsmith, with a background in Fine Art.
COURTESY PAUL YOUNG

The amount of tea I drink on any given day is generally a good indication of my work output. A long or particularly challenging day is peppered with tea breaks. Well, not so much tea breaks as contemplative teatimes, which are usually spent drinking said 'cuppa' at my workbench, while examining work in progress and deciding on the next step. These are pivotal times in the day since, when you are working with metal, once you make your move there is often no way back. In that way it is quite an unforgiving material so it pays to think before you act. As a work colleague used to say to me, 'the quickest way to make a piece of jewellery is to not make any mistakes.'

I'm not too fussy about the brand as long as it has a bit of welly to it. I must admit I find it hard to face a watery cup of milky tea, even when politeness is at risk. If you were to call to my house for tea and a chat you would be imposed upon to administer your own milk and sugar, for Heaven forbid you mess with an Irishman/Irishwoman's tea. As a people, I think we take our tea pretty seriously. Not in the traditional English 'afternoon tea' kind of way with all its bells and whistles but in an altogether more earthy, meaningful way which says, I don't care if you serve it to me in an old boot as long as it's a good cup of tea (and by God, I mean served exactly the way I like it).

I'm not too fussy about the brand as long as it has got a bit of welly to it.

When I was a student in Dublin I was very friendly with a group of Kiwi backpackers who were living in Ireland for a year or so. I remember being invited around for dinner one night, which was a hearty, casual affair with many bodies crammed around the kitchen table. I don't remember what we ate but after dinner I will never forget being served tea in a jam jar. The thought of it still brings a smile to my face. I don't know why it was so enjoyable to drink tea from this unusual vessel but perhaps it was the element of innocent rebellion about it that tickled me.

The Punk Rocker is a miniature decorative teapot created by Yvonne, which won the National Craft competition: Company of Goldsmiths of Dublin Award in August 2012.
COURTESY ROLAND PASCHHOFF

CATHERINE FULVIO

Catherine Fulvio, TV chef and author, runs the award-winning Ballyknocken House and Cookery School in County Wicklow.

COURTESY CATHERINE FULVIO

I remember telling my husband's family, the Fulvios in Sicily, that my granddad would always drink a mug of tea with his dinner. In a country where there are many food rules, drinking tea with your '*secondi*' or main course was not in keeping with tradition.

But I am third generation here at Ballyknocken House. Everything revolved around tea. Supper was 'tea time'. Recycled glass lemonade bottles were filled with sweet milky tea for all the neighbouring farmers, who had come to help get the silage or hay in.

When, over thirty years ago, a Japanese guest to our B&B gave us a gift of green tea, my mother almost passed out from the smell. When a German guest asked to make tea from the camomile in the garden, there were lots of under-breath mutterings about such strange ways. Real tea was Irish breakfast tea. That was more than three decades ago and the previous century.

And when we weren't drinking tea, we were cooking with it. This is my family tea brack recipe. It is one of the easiest recipes in the world and so delicious when it has just cooled. My mother used to bury wrapped coins in the cake, so it got eaten very fast, whether we liked raisins or not, such was the draw of the few coppers hidden inside.

BALLYKNOCKEN TEA BRACK

350 ml/12½ fl oz cold water
540g/1 lb 2 oz sultanas
275g/9 oz sugar
275g/9 oz butter

400g/14 oz self-raising flour
1 tsp/5 ml mixed spice
3 to 4 eggs, beaten

Optional: chopped nuts, glacé cherries mixed into cake

22.5cm/9 inch square cake tin
Preheat the oven to 180°C/300°–350°F/Gas 4
Line the cake tin with greased parchment paper
Wrap trinkets such as coins and rings in parchment paper (as tightly and neatly as possible)
Put the water, fruit, sugar and butter in a saucepan and bring to boil.
Boil for 5–10 minutes. Remove from the heat and allow to cool.
Sieve flour and mixed spice into a large bowl.
When the boiled mixture has cooled, pour into the flour and mix well.
Add beaten eggs and beat well. Pour into the prepared cake tin.
Push the wrapped trinkets into the cake mixture (i.e. below the surface so there is no trace of them when the cake is cooked).
Bake in a preheated moderate oven for approximately 1½ hours. After 30 minutes, reduce oven temperature to 160°C/325°F/Gas 3 for the remainder of the cooking time. Test with a skewer – if skewer is dry, the cake is ready.

(This cake can easily be made without the trinkets. If you are putting the trinkets in, don't forget to forewarn your guests.)

JULIE MELIA

Julie Melia left her TV job and the city for family life in the country, but she still looks forward to every tea break.

Jinny's Kitchen

In my boring office job, I used to love when someone would appear making the letter 'T' with two of their fingers. If they came to your desk it was legit break time. From a distance, saying 'pssssst' generally meant someone was having a bad day or there was major gossip. Occasionally, I'd be summoned by my boss for tea – to make a serious chat seem friendlier. I'd always decline the vending-machine tea, convinced that all beverages came out the same spout.

I worked in RTÉ for ten years and once when I was being trained in on a job in a control room, I was told that the most important thing was to bring my own cup – not which button to press in case of an emergency.

This photo was taken of me while skiving off and sneaking around the old *Glenroe* set in its final days. What else would you do in Dinny's kitchen but have tea? Tea is always time out. The leveller. The person who puts the kettle on at gatherings is the person who has a gift for putting people at ease.

The thoughtful person who insists on making the tea when they visit someone with a new baby can bring that new mother to tears. Whatever the problem, we'll sort it out over a cup of tea.

As a child, I'd love the sound of the kettle boiling downstairs when my parents relieved the babysitter after a night out. I knew they were home and everything was OK. My mother always taught me that if you offered someone tea, you then sat down and had a cup with them, even if you were full of tea already.

It's the little things that put people at ease, that let the chat flow. And it's a small but perfect joy to meet someone who takes their tea the exact same way as you. My husband and I take a tiny drop of milk in tall mugs. However, I'm guilty of hiding biscuits from my husband – to keep in case someone calls in unannounced. He thinks you can offer just tea, but I'm horrified at this idea. It depends on your background. Mine is very much a tea-and-biscuits background.

I love the story of the lady long ago on the Aran Islands who had a priest to visit. A relation had sent her tea leaves and she was keeping the package for such an occasion but she didn't know what to do with it. She gave the priest a plate of boiled tea leaves and a knob of butter on top.

'Ah missus', said the priest, ''Tis the juice I want!'

Whatever the problem, we'll sort it out over a cup of tea

TERRY DONNELLY

Terry Donnelly is a teacher and writer who now lives in Melbourne, Australia.

COURTESY AMBER DONNELLY

I've lived in Melbourne for over three years. It's a mixed bag, being away from Ireland. Different people deal with the distance in different ways. I have friends who still talk about moving 'home' in a few years, when it seems more likely that it's not going to happen. Some Irish in Australia surround themselves with Irish friends, wear the football jersey, go back for every holiday, or weekends revolve around the Irish pubs. I don't know about that way of living. You can be pulled in too many directions at once. Australia is not Ireland, no matter how many Republic of Cork T-shirts you see on St Kilda beach. But while Australia might not be home, Ireland isn't either. I suppose like a lot of people

I'm somewhere between. Yet for all that I always have a box of Barry's on top of the fridge.

Every morning, rising for work as the first trams trundle down Brunswick Street, I boil the kettle for a cup of tea. I've tried other milky teas in Australia, but none of them are up to the job. They're typically too weak, and steeping doesn't make the tea any better, just bitter and unpalatable. My Australian friends ask for it by name when I offer them a cup. It's fun to hear them ask for Barry's, and they all want to solve the mystery of who Barry is. My wife, Amber, a Queenslander, is committed to the cause and even more of an enthusiast than me. She hassles friends of mine who are returning to Ireland to bring out a few boxes on return. When we run low, she gets her emergency supplies from Paddy's Meats, an Irish butcher in Kew, maybe a half an hour's drive from us, traffic depending.

It's not all Barry's though. In the hot weather I might drink Japanese roasted rice green tea, chilled in the fridge. In dumpling houses on Little Bourke Street it's pots and pots of jasmine tea. And sometimes it's sweetened mint tea after dinner, with a piece of baklava. Like a lot of things in Australia, it's a bit of every world here. And the Australians themselves have their own tea rituals. Most important of these is morning tea on special or social occasions. It's similar to morning tea in England or Ireland, but also not quite the same. I've read that the custom was popularised by the Anzacs returning from the First World War. It's a social meal (with tea!) between breakfast and lunch, and typically everyone brings a plate of pastries, cakes or savoury treats. And Melbourne being Melbourne, tea has to compete with the city's obsession with coffee. Well, the Italians were never going to drink tea, were they?

That said, my ritual is sitting at the end of our red gum table every morning and having a cup of Barry's. It's tempting, of course, to say that in the steam off the cup I see the mist rolling in off Mizen Head, or in the rust-red pour I see the colours of bog streams flowing down from Lugnaquilla. Maybe it's there, but mostly I'm just waking up. Sentiment is seductive, but it can cloud perception. A friend of mine

What does Irish tea tell us about the Irish? It's strongly flavoured and colourful.

was in an Irish bar here in Melbourne with a Chinese friend. They went up to the barman and the Chinese guy asked the barman if he had any tea. Yes, he was told. What type of tea, he asked. Irish tea, the barman replied incredulously. The Chinese guy turned to my friend in puzzlement. 'I didn't know you grew tea in Ireland.'

Tea isn't an Irish thing, of course, it's universal. But tea isn't just another food item either. It's a cultural staple, like bread, beer or cheese, and as such it contains custom and therefore meaning about who a people are. So what does Irish tea tell us about the Irish? It's strongly flavoured and colourful. It's down to earth and not too fancy. People are peculiar about how they like it. It doesn't change much, so it's not subject to fads or fashions.

My mate Ger, from east Cork, calls to our house for dinner every so often. Afterwards we have a cup of tea and talk about work, life, family, the weekend, the meaning of the universe and so on. In doing this we're taking a break. We're putting our feet up, not running around being absorbed by time, by media, by the city. The most culturally obvious aspect of Irish tea is that it brings people together for a chat, for a bit of balm and banter. It's not really the place, and maybe it's not even the type of tea. Like Yeats' dancer and the dance, it can't be rationalised or deconstructed. The magic occurs as it happens. I'd like to think, by some mysterious process, that when we're drinking tea we're ourselves again. We're not separate or foreign, we're not pulled between. In Ger's east Cork lilt, as the milk is poured, I'm suddenly home again. Sipping breakfast tea with Amber, while morning brightens the night sky, I find that I belong.

Haines sat down to pour out the tea.

– I'm giving you two lumps each, he said. But, I say, Mulligan, you do make strong tea, don't you?

Buck Mulligan, hewing thick slices from the loaf, said in an old woman's wheedling voice:

– When I makes tea I makes tea, as old mother Grogan said. And when I makes water I makes water.

– By Jove, it is tea, Haines said.

Buck Mulligan went on hewing and wheedling:

– So I do, Mrs Cahill, says she. Begob, ma'am, says Mrs Cahill, God send you don't make them in the one pot.

ULYSSES, JAMES JOYCE

MOIRA BEHAN

Moira Behan, from County Kildare, worked as Night Superintending Nurse at Naas Hospital for thirty-four years. She now enjoys jigsaws, bowls and walking.

I do love a cup of tea. I don't have a favourite mug but I do like tea in a mug. I like it with a little milk, fairly strong, and with sugar. I can't go without sugar in my tea. I've tried giving it up for Lent and I just couldn't. It was easier giving up smoking than to give up sugar in my tea. The cup of tea and the fag went hand in hand, but about twenty years ago, I quit smoking forty fags a day, just like that. I had no problem giving up cigarettes, but I can't give up the sugar in the tea.

I worked as Night Superintending Nurse over Naas Hospital for over thirty years. In all that time, only six months were spent on day shifts, the rest was night duty. Things have changed down through the years. Back in the 1970s, patients were free to go into the kitchen themselves and make a cup of tea. Or I would make them a cup of tea at night time and they'd always look forward to the cuppa before they'd settle down. Then maybe on a night you would be busy and you wouldn't get time, they might complain about not getting the tea. It was very important to them.

I found the cup of tea really important for patients if they were awake during the night. Sometimes they are awake because they're troubled about something and oftentimes with the cup of tea and the chat they come out with what's bothering them, and once they've unloaded it to someone else it settles them down. The cup of tea and chat was better than any sleeping tablet.

In later years, they didn't let patients into the kitchen because of health and safety, and in latter years nurses weren't allowed to make the tea, it was care assistants, so you didn't have that same opportunity to chat. I think that was a pity.

Part of my job was to deliver bad news and the tea was very much part of that, even though people just drank it automatically. Tea was something to offer while you chatted to those people. I was either the person who broke the news that their loved one had passed away or you were the first in line, after the doctor broke the news, and you stayed with the people, just to be there with them if they had any questions or if they had to be taken to the mortuary.

It certainly put a lot of things in perspective doing that job. At the time, you feel it very much for the person or family you're with, and you almost cry with them, but once you come outside that door in the morning you have to leave it behind or you couldn't do the job. Unfortunately, bad news and tragedy were just too regular – you'd be a wreck if you dwelled on it all.

Coffee was seen as a yuppie thing, years ago. Even today, fewer people ask for coffee. I play bowling now, and on our bowling nights we make tea and you might have only one person having a cup of coffee or just one for a cup of hot water and the rest would drink tea. At bowls competitions, the cup of tea and sandwiches after the game are very important and it's a lovely way of meeting people from other clubs. During the competition you're serious about competing, but afterwards it's a real social thing.

I also play pitch and putt and after our own little competitions in the evening, we go into the clubhouse for a cup of tea. When we go to Spain on holidays, we bring teabags but when we go on cruises we don't, they'd have all sorts of brands on board, even Bewleys.

I drink about eight cups of tea a day, but not late at night. My last would be around eight o'clock, but if I couldn't sleep or if I woke up at 5 a.m. and couldn't get back to sleep, I might get up and make a cup of tea and a piece of toast.

Below: Brownstown Bowls Club enjoy a great spread after a game against Coill Dubh, in Brownstown Community Hall, The Curragh, County Kildare. Back row (l–r): Lily Higgins, Moira Behan, Michael McMahon, Mary Stynes, Antoinnette Doyle, Kevin Doyle, Ailish Vardy, Frank Breen; front row (l–r): Murt Synott, Ann Hunter, Betty Gannon, Claire Breen, Christy Flynn, Cathal Malone.

Facing page: Refreshments after the competition.

CATHY KELLY

Cathy Kelly is a number one best-selling author. She worked as a journalist before becoming a novelist and has published fifteen novels. She is also an ambassador for UNICEF in Ireland. She lives in County Wicklow with her husband and two sons.
www.cathykelly.com

COURTESY SARAH CONROY

How do you take your tea?
Weak, with sugar and a smidge of milk. I can't stand milky tea.

How many cups per day?
Not many – I start with coffee and have perhaps three cups of tea. Tea and biscuits in the evening is heaven.

Do you have a favourite brand?
No.

Do you take Irish teabags abroad with you when you travel?
When I do big tours, yes!

When did you start drinking tea?
I think I must have started when I was very small as I spent all of my childhood summers with my grandmother and she was mad for strong tea. I can remember great sessions in my nana's house years ago when people would drop in. The pot would be put on the old black range, tea would be stewed to a rich peaty colour and great chat would emerge over tea and my grandmother's currant cake.

Do you have a favourite cup?
The cup is SO important. In my family, I am known for my oddity surrounding cups. I don't like big jorums of tea or coffee – just small, perfect ones. I used to have a lovely brown, curvy, small mug (I saw the exact same one on an American TV show lately and shrieked with joy) but it broke, so my current favourites are two small, black, octagonal mugs from the 1980s. If they are not available, I have to look into the cupboard and think hard.

Why do Irish people like tea so much?
Tea is one of the answers to the problems of the universe. At all great moments of disaster, a moment of calm can be had by making a cup of tea. It allows us all time to think and collect ourselves during the hubbub of getting out the cups and milk.

Tea is one of the answers to the problems of the universe.

BERTHA HINCH

Bertha Hinch was born on 23 May 1920. Bertha has eight children, twenty-one grandchildren and two great-grandchildren. She lives in Oldcourt, Blessington, County Wicklow.

I love tea. Years ago, I used to work in a dairy and grocery shop, on the East Wall in Dublin, and we used to weigh out the tea from big tea chests. I was there at the time of the rations during the war, and each customer was only allowed their ration of a half ounce. But the real Dublin men who used to work on the docks, their tea would run out after a day or two. We would open at seven o'clock in the morning, and they'd come in for their milk. They couldn't have the food in their house at night because if they did it would be gone by morning. The kids would have it eaten, coming home from the pictures. So often the wives would come early and they'd ask, 'would you give us an ounce out of the rations to get me husband out to work?' Of course you would give it to them but you weren't meant to. During the war, they made a drink out of cocoa shell when the tea was gone. With all the rationing I felt sorry for the people so I gave up sugar in my tea. No one had much then, but everybody got through it anyway.

We stayed around the corner, in the shop owner's front room. Anywhere you worked, you lived in. The shop would be open until all hours and you'd have to walk up the street with the day's takings, but you'd feel safe. My first job, at about fourteen years of age, was in Horan's shop, off Henry Cole's Lane. Then I went to work for Kelly's of the Coombe, who owned a few shops. I worked in Pimlico and then Ormond Quay which was very convenient for Mass across the bridge in Merchant's Quay. Kelly's had a tea room on Ormond Quay as a lot of people would be walking from Heuston Station.

Dairy and grocery shops sold all the necessities: fruit, vegetables, tea, sugar, creamery butter, salt and pepper. Farmers would bring two or three churns of milk to the shop and the milk would have to be tilted over into an earthenware crock and put on the shop counter. People would come in and out all day for a pint or a quart of milk. They'd bring a jug and the milk would be measured into it. You had quart and pint measures hanging up. It was three pence a pint and sixpence a quart, and an inspector would come around once a year to make sure all the measures were right.

Butter would come in timber boxes, about 28 lb. It would have to be cut into 2 oz or ¼ lb blocks and wrapped in greaseproof paper. The box was very useful, as it could be made into seats. Sugar came in a big sack. We bought butter paper and sugar bags, 2 lb and 1 lb, in Evans' shop in Mary's Lane. The sugar would be weighed up and put into these bags and fastened. People would come for 2 oz of butter in the morning and then come back later to get another 2 oz maybe. The tea was weighed in the same way as the sugar.

Then I worked for Hibernian Dairies, who had stores on Pearse St, Hanlon's Corner, and Church Road, East Wall. They were all painted yellow. We would make our own meals at the shop. The shop would open at 7 a.m. and my friend with whom I worked and I would go to Mass at 9 a.m. on alternate days.

I had a bicycle at home in Saggart and I remember cycling to East Wall from Saggart. I worked with Margaret O'Brien and on our half day off we often went to her sister's in North Strand. We'd spend the afternoon knitting. Clothes were rationed and it was important to be able to make your own garments. I remember cycling to Guiney's on Talbot Street for nylons, which were rationed. Whenever I got a day off, I went home to Saggart.

The gas was rationed as well, so your gas was regularly turned off, but there was always a glimmer. And if you put a kettle on it, it would boil eventually. There used to be a man they called the 'Glimmerman' who'd go around watching, in case you were using the gas, so you could get in trouble with the glimmerman.

Back then, nobody ever got out and marched for anything that was taken off them. It's not like today: if people are deprived of anything today they go marching. You just accepted it back then.

At a later stage, I worked for O'Gorman's on Connaught St, Phibsborough. I was sleeping there the night of the bombing of the North Strand. I went up to my room and, on the stairs at midnight, I heard a noise. A man on the street outside shouted, 'Put out the lights, put out the lights.' I went up and sat on the bed while the windows rattled. When the noise stopped, people gathered in the shop to talk. We heard about people going across Newcomen Bridge and being blown up. Between Amiens Street and the Five Lamps, all the houses were demolished. Many people were only coming home from the pictures at the time. There was no warning. A big crater appeared in the road at

the bottom of Dorset St and the end of the North Circular Road. It was 31 May 1941. We had been trained to use gas masks and dugouts in the event of an attack, but there was no warning so we weren't ready.

We heard the bombers coming overhead. They went down North Circular Road and William St, and North Strand. There were butchers and all down there, there would have been children coming home to find their houses gone, because it all happened at about midnight, when they were coming home from town. The German Luftwaffe dropped four bombs on the North Strand area, killing thirty-four people and injuring ninety. Some 300 houses were damaged or destroyed. I was awake all night.

In the 1940s, I used to always have a pain in my shoulder. I thought it was from driving, and I remember going to this arthritis seminar in a hotel on O'Connell St and it was all about tea. Dr Alexander was the speaker's name, over from America, and he was giving a talk about the tea and how bad it was for you and that it was the cause of arthritis and all this. He said he was disgusted by how much tea the Irish drank. Dr Alexander said he was going to bring so many chests of tea to O'Connell Bridge and throw them all into the Liffey. He said, 'I'm going to unload them into the Liffey in front of you all.' The women all knew the day he was going to do this and they went down and brought their shopping bags and their prams and their kids, and when they saw the tea chests being taken off the lorry at O'Connell Bridge, they filled their bags with tea before it landed in the water. No matter how bad the tea was for them they still wanted it!

When we were children, on our farm, we had no taps: we had to fetch water across the fields. We were always carrying water. We'd go down to the river and bring two buckets, balanced across our shoulders on a brush handle. We were never left idle, making butter and carrying water. You were glad to go to school to get away from the work. I remember my mother used to sing when she was sitting under the cows, milking. We would have to feed all the pigs and cows. We had a big churn for the butter in the kitchen. I was always left at home and had to do the work. My sister May used to slip away and you'd find her behind a cock of hay with a book.

We had big drills of turnips to dig and to weed, and when school started in September, we'd have to stay at home and pick the potatoes. There wasn't that much sickness, though, then. You were always busy. You might get a penny bar for doing all the drills. It's all changed now, it's all money now. It wasn't all about money then. But there are a lot of great things now if they were appreciated.

Eventually, about 1956, Fr Collins, a local priest, organised the water scheme and arranged for us to get water in the house. We got the electricity in 1950. We used to have a bath for washing clothes and nappies. You had a big bucket for softening the nappies and then you'd wash them later. Everyone was put to bed early because you had to get the washing done while the children were asleep.

> *We used to use the empty tea chests as a playpen for the smallest baby in the house.*

We used to use the empty tea chests as a playpen for the smallest baby in the house. They were safe in there while you were doing something. And you wouldn't have to be buying them things all the time to play with. You could throw them in an old box and they'd love playing with that – they could make things out of it and get in and out of it. I wouldn't have been able to do anything without a tea chest to put the baby in. When they were older, the children were always outside playing until dark – there was no room for them in the house. I wouldn't have given tea to the children when they were young, but they all drink tea now.

My mother used to go over and visit a woman who lived nearby and she'd always say, 'Will you have a cup of tea? Sure, you won't, you're only after having a cup.' She would answer for you before you got the chance to say 'yes'. Anyone who comes to my house always has a cup of tea. Everybody loves a cup of tea.

Waterford Dramatic Society, 1950s.

PODGE AND RODGE

Podge and Rodge are Ballydung's most eligible bachelors.
COURTESY DOUBLE Z ENTERPRISES

How do you take your tea?

Rodge: Using my hands.

Podge: You really are a gobsheen; do you not understand anything? I like my tea like I like my women: hot and sweet.

Rodge: Oh I get it, I can do that! I like my tea like I like my women: in a cup with a biscuit on the side.

Podge: Give me strength.

How many cups per day?

Podge: As many as I can get Rodge to make me.

Rodge: About ten. I need the caffeine for all the running around making Podge's tea.

Do you have a favourite brand?

Podge: Barry's or Lyons.

Rodge: We dry them out in the hot press and re-use them.

Podge: Both those brands have a high re-usability factor.

Do you take Irish teabags abroad when you travel?

Podge: We took some up to Dublin when we came for the shopping on 8 December last year, but it turned out ponces drink tea too!

When did you start drinking tea?

Rodge: Like all Irish farmers, in a bottle, aged three months.

Any memorable moments accompanied by tea?

Podge: Magical midget Paul Daniels almost threw a cup of tea over us once.

Rodge: Did he like us? Not a lot!

Podge: Best would be the many cups of tea we've shared with some of the hottest women in Ireland – Kennedy (Lucy and Mary), Seoige (both), Morahan, Thomas, Doyle and O'Callaghan.

Do you have a favourite mug?

Podge: Mine's an old one I got at a cattle mart. It's so stained now but Granny always said you should never wash a teapot or a mug.

Rodge: I have one with a lady in a bikini on it and when you put anything hot into it, the bikini disappears. I sometimes just leave it on the radiator ...

Have you any stories about tea drinking?

Podge: No. That would be boring.

Rodge: You can't tell stories about tea!

Podge: Next you'll be telling us someone's bringing out a book about it. Stories about tea!! Have you ever heard the like?

Why do Irish people like tea so much?

Podge: We're not a pretentious people like the French or Italians. All of that fancy coffee nonsense. Latte-dahs, Gestapochinos and George Clooney and his tiny cups.

Rodge: There's only two questions to ask with tea – milk and sugar?

Podge: Exactly. It's no nonsense, just like the Irish.

LAURA UGBEBOR

Laura Ugbebor is fifteen years old and is a transition year student at Holy Family Community School, Rathcoole, County Dublin.

I started drinking tea when I was five or six. My mam didn't want me drinking caffeine so she just buys decaf tea. She loves tea. I always make her a cup of tea when she gets in from work. I see her face and I know she's tired from the day, so I make her tea. I just take milk, no sugar, and I drink decaf, camomile or green tea. Lots of teenagers drink tea. Before afterschool study here in the school, lots of students buy tea in the little school shop. My mum is a social worker so she studied a lot – I think that's when she started drinking a lot of tea, to help her study late into the night.

I like a big mug because I can bring that upstairs when I'm doing homework or studying and it saves me the effort of coming back downstairs and making more. If my little sister makes me tea she knows to use my Homer Simpson mug because it's nice and big.

If I'm not feeling well or if something's happened, I always say, 'just let me have a cup of tea', thinking it would make it better. Tea is something you can always fall back on.

Patrick Higgins feeding his sheep in the depths of winter on the Curragh Plains.

KATHLEEN CULLEN

Kathleen Cullen lives with her husband, Des, in Manor Kilbride, County Wicklow. They have been playing cards with their neighbours and friends each week since 1958. The tea is a very important part of their card-playing evenings. As Des explains, 'we concentrate during the game and it's very serious, but we have great fun during the tea breaks.'

My mother was the biggest tea drinker I've ever known. When tea was scarce during the war, she got this special spoon that had a clip-on cover with holes on it, an infuser. It held a spoonful of tea and she could use the same tea leaves again. She always had a ceramic teapot – she said the tea wasn't the same from aluminium teapots. She always made tea cosies and that's how I came to make them myself. She would have the teapot on the table and a big, thick tea cosy over it and it would stay hot for ages. I've knitted tea cosies from scraps of wool, but real sheep's wool, so they are really thick. Years ago, everybody had a tea cosy for the good teapot. I suppose nowadays people use the stainless steel teapots and they stay warm, but I'm like my mother, I never had an aluminium teapot. I think the tea tastes different.

'Have a cup of tea' was the first thing my mother would say when anyone came in at home. She loved getting a nice tea for someone: she pulled out all the stops. I remember she'd always have the china cup for the local teacher when she visited. She had a collection of teapots on the top shelf of the dresser at home. She must have collected them early on, she had half a dozen old teapots up on the dresser, and the lid always broke so you were left with this teapot with no lid and it was an ornament then. It might be full of notes or little messages or goodness knows what.

My mother ran a shop. It was just beside the church, and people used to walk to Mass on First Friday, maybe from Ballyfolan, four or five miles away, and they'd all have been fasting from the night before, so my mother would have this army of women in making tea and toast. The toast would have to be done at the fire with a big long fork. They'd come in after Mass and have their tea and toast and they'd walk home then. These were all friends of hers. She'd set the table and have the china cups out. My mother wouldn't drink out of a mug in a million years, not even when she was living here with us, she hated mugs. It would have to be a dainty cup.

During the war, there was the carry-on over the ration coupons. My mother wouldn't have the coupons to correspond with the tea she gave out, because she gave the tea to the people who needed it, who had children, even if they had used their rations. Eventually she was hauled in to the Department of Industry and Commerce because her returns didn't tally with the amount of tea she had given out so she was in serious trouble with them. They were going to prosecute her at one stage. She got out of it in the end but I don't know how.

The Black Market for tea during the war was something else: a pound for a pound of tea – it should have cost maybe

The Black Market for tea during the war was something else: a pound for a pound of tea

2 shillings for 1 lb of tea and they were charging £1 for it, and people were buying it. My mother even paid that for it, because she had to have tea. She loved it. She always said there was nothing like it for the thirst. The men would be out making hay in the fields and she used to make the tea in big three-quart cans that we used to get in the shop for boiled sweets. In good sunny weather we children would be sent out with this tea in the three-quart can, with the lid on it, and sandwiches and cups in a bag, to the men in the fields. Sure tea never tasted like it, it was brilliant. They'd have loads of it, the can of tea with the milk and sugar all in it, of course. The men would sit down at the bottom of the cock of hay and have their tea.

When the war was over in the 1940s, the delivery system was bad and we'd go in on the bus to this place, Hoggs, on Cope St, who were tea merchants, and you'd bring home this big parcel of tea on the bus. Pattisons on Thomas St was another place. There were lots of different tea merchants then, and a lot of the pubs had 'wine and tea' written up outside.

A group of us play cards in each other's homes once a week and a big part of the card playing is the tea. There are nine of us, so I have to use a couple of teapots because mine are the small ceramic pots. It's a good old pastime. We always have the tea when we're playing cards, at least once; we might even have a second round before we go home. One woman makes pavlovas for us and they're gorgeous.

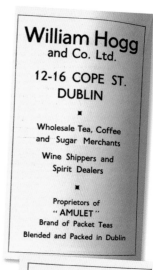

Pictured at a card game in Kathleen's house, clockwise from left: Tom Brady, Seamus Cummins, Paddy Quinn, Michael Kearns, Des Cullen, Peter Clarke, Mary Clarke, Tess Cummins and Kathleen Cullen.

I couldn't drink tea when I was expecting a baby – it made me sick – but I could drink coffee. Even the smell of the tea would have me running to the bathroom. But as soon as the child was born, I could drink away at the tea again.

A nun told me that one year for Lent, her Reverend Mother told all the nuns in the convent to give up sugar in their tea, which they did, and of course, after Lent they all stayed off the sugar because they didn't like it any more. But the following year the Reverend Mother told them to take the sugar in their tea for Lent – as penance. She said that was ten times worse.

I don't like very strong tea, just medium strength. My mother used to look at my tea and say 'That's innocent water scalded.'

I know of one woman who was always going around with a cup of tea: you never saw her in her house without a cup of tea in her hand. She loved her tea so much that when she died, they left a cup of tea beside her coffin when she was laid out up in the house.

DUNGARVAN MEN'S SHED

Fun over 'Gerry's tea' at Dungarvan Men's Shed, County Waterford, every Tuesday and Thursday morning. Back row (l–r): Tony Walsh, Frank McClintock, David Casey aka 'Skerries', Tommy Butler, Liam Douglas, Martin Waters, and Pat O'Mahoney; front row (l–r): Nicky Sheehan, Michael French, Eddie Bennett, Tom O'Mahony, Paddy McNamara, and John Foley.

NICKY SHEEHAN

Nicky Sheehan is Deputy Lord Mayor of Dungarvan and a founder member of Dungarvan Men's Shed.

I love tea. I worked in the glass factory for thirty-four years, and you drank tea on your breaks, twice a day, but since the factory closed, it's tea, tea, tea! I don't know whether it's a crutch to lean on or what. I've recently changed over to decaf tea at home because I'm drinking so much of it, and the decaf usually does the job, but I break the rules when I come to the Men's Shed.

In May 2012, myself and Michael Cass and Brendan Hally set up Dungarvan Men's Shed. We were like the lads from *Last of the Summer Wine*. I was sitting at home one night and I was thinking about all the people like me, whose jobs and factories and businesses have closed down, all the men put on the scrap heap, for want of a better word. We wanted to do something. So we went off on a jaunt one day around Cork and we saw the Men's Shed in Youghal, so we took a notion to create our own shed and thanks be to God it worked out for us and it has gone from strength to strength. It's such an important place for me, inside in that shed. Most of the lads – men who retired or are unemployed – they lost a lot. What I miss most, in fact, is the camaraderie. You go from having friends and work colleagues and enjoying great chats every day over your tea breaks to losing all those connections with other people. The Men's Shed has rekindled that for people. A lot of lads who aren't originally from Dungarvan say they have made more friends in the last month since they joined the shed than they did in all the years they lived here. The first thing you do when you come in here is put on the kettle and have an aul' cup of tea.

DAVID CASEY

After twenty years working on fishing trawlers, David Casey, aka 'Skerries', worked on the lifeboats in Waterford for ten years. He lives in Dungarvan and is a regular at Dungarvan Men's Shed.

They call me Skerries because that's where I grew up. I went to sea when I was eleven, during school holidays. My father left the house when I was eight and I had three younger sisters so I had to do something. I went to sea full time at thirteen. I had to leave school but it meant I brought money into the house. Until then, we had no electricity, we had no television, no radio, no nothing, and when I went fishing, everything changed. When I was fourteen or so, I was bringing home £500 or £600 a week – savage money. My mother always thanked me for doing what I did.

When we went to sea, we had to bring everything with us: water, bread, milk, rashers, sausages, eggs, and, of course, tea. Tea was very important. We used to bring plastic drums of water with us and if you forgot to fill them up before you left, the racket would quickly start if there was no water for tea. We always had fish and spuds for dinner. It was all boiled in salt water, scooped in over the side of the boat – that was the nicest thing ever.

Sometimes when you were out fishing for a few days, you'd run out of tea. If you were stuck, each of you was allocated just one teabag to get you through the rest of the time.

Fishing from Helvick, you could spend five days at sea. That's tough. It's like being in prison. You were confined to this small space. You had to trust the skipper and the other crewmen and they had to trust you. From eleven o'clock at night until six in the morning, I'd be the one behind the wheel, so the boat and its crew were my responsibility. The crew were asleep in their bunks, so if I nodded off, anything could happen. You had to have friendship and trust to work together, because if you didn't, all it takes is one push and you're gone.

I used to fish with a fella from Loughshinny and he used to be blaggarding while he was making the tea. When the kettle was boiled, he'd take it off the cooker and he'd put it on his hand and he'd tell you to hold it there until he said 'go', to pour. His eyes wouldn't even water, he had skin like leather and his fingers were all crooked. At that time, all the heavy work on the boat had to be done by hand. The drum end on the big winch had the ropes coming off it, and you had to catch every coil of rope that came off the drum in your hands and stack them. His hands got tough from that, and he couldn't feel anything any more.

But he'd hold the kettle on his bare hand and laugh.

I always say the nicest cup of tea I ever tasted was made with tea leaves in the old teapot in my grandmother's

> *The nicest cup of tea I ever tasted was made with tea leaves in the old teapot in my grandmother's house*

house, in Rush. And the homemade brown bread and the 'currany' cake, as we used to call it. I was probably about six when I started drinking tea – although it was mostly milk. We were given Guinness in milk, too, back then.

It's good aul' craic in the Men's Shed. We drink a lot of tea and make a lot of new friends. There are projects you can help out on. We're renovating five workshops at the moment, so we're going to have a welding shop, metalwork, woodwork, craftwork, and painting. Someone's pledged a pool table and we're putting in our own kitchen and doing all the work ourselves. It's great to be involved and it's a very positive place to be.

TOMMY BUTLER

Tommy Butler, served for twenty-two years in the Irish Defence Forces, based in Collins Barracks, Cork.

I joined the army in 1962. The tae that time was leaves in big huge bags. The tea vats were huge – they were making tea for maybe 500 people. You could get chefs that couldn't make tea – there could be socks and all inside in it. The food when I started off in the army was terrible. The cooks would go in at four or five o'clock in the morning and boil the eggs for the breakfast, and you could throw them down to the end of the dining hall and they wouldn't break. They'd been boiling for about six hours! Fellas in the army, they'd eat anything. I remember when I joined the army, I wouldn't eat carrots, and I wouldn't eat this and that. After three weeks, I'd have eaten the table. Hunger is a great sauce.

But the food in the army nowadays is excellent. And it was good when we were overseas. I did twelve months in Cyprus with the army. That was the first time the Irish army ever went anywhere with sun. The first time we went there, it was October and it was about 40 degrees. We didn't know what the heat was. I remember the first day, we all lay out in the sun. We were destroyed! And there's two things in the army you got fined for – sunburn and ingrown toenails, because that's self-neglect. If you're out sick with sunburn, you won't get paid.

The army brought tea out to Cyprus with us. Because the food was good there, I remember we'd come back to the table, with plates piled high, up to eye level. The boss man would come along and say to us, 'I don't care what you take, but what you take, you eat.' There was no waste.

In Cyprus, one town would be a Greek town and the next might be a Turkish town, but out the country the farmers might be next door to one another, so we had to escort the vet out around the villages. The farmers brought all their cattle into the village and we had to wait while the vet inoculated them. Each village had their own boss man, the 'mukhtar' they called him, and in each village the mukhtar would give us soldiers Turkish tea in a small little cup. And they'd have you drinking this all day. Real Turkish tea is like tar. And each village you went to was the same – and you might do six or seven villages in a day. But you had to drink it or you'd insult them. Thank God they were small cups. It was a terrible laxative. You'd be coming down the mountain and you'd hit a bump on the road and you'd have to shout, 'Stop! Stop!'

ANNE GILDEA

Anne Gildea is a Dublin-based writer and performer. Anne is a member of The Nualas, one of the most successful all-girl, shiny-dressed, unbelievably sexy, big-boned, harmonising comedy acts to ever come out of Ireland. Ever.

COURTESY BRENDAN DEMPSEY

(L-r): Sue Collins, Maria Tecce and Anne Gildea, aka The Nualas.

COURTESY MARK NEILAND

I love my tea. I drink gallons of tea when I'm writing. I have a pot of coffee first, then move on to tea so I don't get too jittery. I drink about five mugs a day, and if I wake in the night I'll get a cup of tea.

I like Earl Grey – all the time – and I like it very strong with a tiny bit of milk. My favourite is Twinings. My mum is a big tea drinker and loves Barry's. She lives in Manchester and we have to bring a big box of Barry's Gold every time we visit. She always stirs the teapot and has to have an extra teabag when she's having tea in a café.

I owned a car once, and I was picking up my mum from the airport and she was talking, talking, talking and I got distracted and a car crashed into me and then my car crashed into another car and another car, and there were five cars involved. My car was a total write-off, and I was in absolute shock. We were waiting for the salvage people to come so we went to a café. My mum sat down in the café and she said, in a dramatic way, 'oh I think I need a cup of tea' and then she put her hand on her chest and her lip began to quiver and she said, 'I think I'm going to cry'. At just that moment, the waitress brought the tea and my mother quickly opened the lid of the teapot and said to her, back to her normal strong voice, 'I need another bag in that pot.' The shock wasn't going to stop her getting her tea the right way!

When we moved to Ireland I was about six and I remember drinking tea from these little green plastic mugs with the other kids. I also remember bottles of tea. I grew up in Sligo and would help out in the hayfield, making cocks of hay the old fashioned way. It was very labour intensive and I clearly remember the smell of hay and that feeling on really hot days, sitting beside a cock of hay, on the prickly ground, having a sandwich and drinking tea from a MiWadi bottle.

I used to bring a flask of tea to primary school. We were driven to school by my aunt, who was a teacher there. She had to stay on late after school, so we had a very long day, and were always given a flask of tea between us. Because we came from tea-loving people they thought we couldn't survive a day without a hot drink. The flasks back then had fragile inserts and they always broke. I was the older sister so I had responsibility for the flask and would have to share the tea with my younger sister Una at break time. I'd follow her around saying, 'I have the flask of tea' and she always remembers this day when I hit her over the head with the flask because she didn't come for her tea, and of course it broke. It's something we always laugh at now. I'm usually very placid.

When I think about it, the tea was so important. We were trained for tea. It would feel a bit weird now offering tea to a five- or six-year-old.

In 2011, I was diagnosed with breast cancer and had a mastectomy and chemotherapy. After I had the biopsy, I was in a lot of pain, which was really startling because I hadn't expected it. The first thing I did was get a cup of tea in the café in St James's Hospital. I used to go there a lot in the following months, during treatment, because they had very nice Earl Grey in these little cloth bags.

That morning I was having all these tests and it was suddenly a bit serious, and the first thing I did when I got away from the tests was to sit down and have a cup of tea.

Also I remember during my chemotherapy, there was a tea lady who came round with tea on the chemotherapy day ward. My sister Una used to come in and keep me company and we would share the one cup of tea. You are in there for three hours at a time, so I loved that, the lovely tea lady coming along. Your tea, and a little biscuit if you wanted, or a sandwich. It made it very pleasant – a bit like being in a hairdresser's. It was very calm in the oncology day ward and a very comfortable, nice atmosphere. I heard women saying that they missed it when the chemo was over. You don't have such an ongoing connection when you're doing radiotherapy. You're just in and out all the time. When you are in the chemo you are in there for hours and you get to know other patients and the nurses. It sounds mad to say it, but you miss that. The ethos in James's is wonderful.

I think we love tea because Irish people are such great talkers and the tea goes with the chat. I always like a hot drink before a show, especially when we are on the road with the Nualas: tea and a sandwich. There's nothing nicer than someone offering you a cup of tea – you know you're at a nice theatre, it's such a welcome. You might have been driving for three hours, you have to do a sound check, change, do the show, get on the road again. It's just lovely if they have facilities there to offer a cup of tea. It makes such a difference. I'll even sometimes have a cup of tea when I come home after a gig. I often go to bed with a cup of tea and read for a while. In fact, I've just realised I drink tea all the time. Tea is always on the horizon when I'm awake … perhaps I drink too much tea.

CELINA ZAJAC

Celina Zajac is an office administrator and lives with her husband, Patryk, and three-year-old daughter Martyna in County Cork.

Paddy the Pole, Martyna, and Celina Zajac.

COURTESY PAWEL FOLTYN

We are originally from Poland, but moved to Ireland in 2003. A tradition we find similar in both our countries is enjoying tea with family, friends and work colleagues. We believe Ireland is number one in Europe for their obsession with drinking tea and Poland is probably close behind.

I met Paddy (originally Patrycjusz) in secondary school in Poland: we were childhood sweethearts, as they say. We got married in September 2002 and after a few days' break in our home town of Czechowice-Dziedzice, in the south of Poland, we went back to work. After six months, we decided to go abroad for a few months to experience a different culture. So we came to Ireland and at the time we called it our honeymoon as we had never had one.

We found jobs during our first week here, living in beautiful Kinsale, County Cork, and we were so happy. Our dreams were already coming true. We were planning to stay up to three months, but then we extended our stay to six months and subsequently to one year. Then Poland joined the EU and it became possible for us to stay in Ireland longer. We bought a house in County Cork and in 2009 our beloved daughter Martyna was born. Now I'd say we are going to stay for good – on our never-ending 'honeymoon'.

In Poland we used to drink tea quite weak, usually with a slice of lemon and two spoons of sugar. Just as in Ireland, the tastiest tea was always in the family home where there was a bit more time for preparation and there was someone to share a cup with. First we prepare what we call the essence or extract. The tea needs to be placed in the small pot and covered with hot water, left for few minutes to develop aroma, taste and colour. Then in the glass teacup, we pour a bit of extract and cover the rest of the cup with hot water. The tea tastes best in the thin glass, far better than in thick glass, a mug or a china cup. Finally add your favourites: sugar, lemon or sometimes milk or honey. We used Lipton, Tetley and Assam tea.

Paddy and I think we actually both started drinking tea very, very early, when we were in our mothers' wombs, as our mothers drank so much tea … and when we were born we had tea on a daily basis 'served' with mother's milk. Those days are well gone but we still drink tea like most Polish and Irish people. We drink three cups of tea each day and even more at weekends. It is simple: we just love it. Tea is a must!

When we moved to Ireland we began integrating with the Irish community and experiencing Irish traditions and sharing our own. When we were asked 'would you like a cup of scald?' for the first time, Paddy and I looked at each other not knowing what to expect. We patiently waited and were surprised to discover a 'cup of scald' was a very nice cup of Irish tea. 'Yes, thank God,' we thought, 'the tea is nice.'

We replaced our thin glass teacups with mugs and the tea tastes absolutely fabulous, too. We no longer prepare extract any more but use our favourite Irish tea, Barry's Original blend. Now we make strong tea directly in scalded cups or in the teapot when we have visitors, and just add milk, and sometimes sugar, depending on the mood. Irish tea tastes nice with a piece of cake but having cake three or more times a day would be a bit too much. Nowadays, every time we go back to Poland to visit our families my dad asks me to bring him Barry's tea.

The tradition of drinking tea in our house is alive and well. We say 'TEA means HOME'. Whether we are in Ireland or in Poland there is always a nice cup of tea to share with family and friends.

Smacznej herbatki – enjoy your tea!

DECLAN EGAN

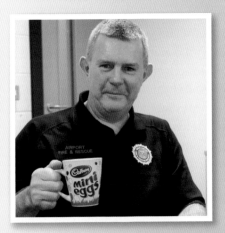

Declan Egan, from Dublin, joined the Airport Police Fire Service in 1979 and has drunk quite a lot of tea since then.

Declan Egan with his favourite mug for work.

I'm the only one left in the fire station who uses tea leaves. The others slag me about how I make my tea. We have a Burco and it's supposed to be boiling water, but it's not. So I use the water that comes from the Burco to fill the kettle and they always say 'oh, you're boiling the boiling water, are you?' and I say 'Yes, I am'.

I learned as a child that to make tea properly, you had to use boiling water. Just as the kettle boiled, you poured a little into the teapot to heat the pot. Then you put in the tea, two or three spoonfuls, depending on the size of the pot. Then you put it sitting on the gas for five minutes to let it draw. But you have to be careful. You see some people putting the teapot back on the ring and they boil it. It has a terrible taste then. After five minutes, you poured a little drop into the sink. I'm not 100 per cent sure what that was about. It might have been to check the colour or if there were leaves stuck in the spout, to let them out first. My father would always check everyone's cup to make sure the milk was in first. It was a military manoeuvre. Milk first, and then you could pour out the tea. In my family, if bubbles formed on top as your tea was poured, they'd say 'that's a sign you're going to get money'. I'm fifty-five now and I've seen plenty of bubbles, but no money!

I grew up near Hanlon's Corner off the North Circular Road, in Dublin, but my parents were from Offaly. I was always brought down to Offaly for the summer and you'd be working out on the bog or out saving hay on the Shannon Callows and an aunt of mine would bring sandwiches and glass bottles filled with tea. It would have milk and sugar in the bottle, and the top would be stuffed with paper. But the tea on the bog was the best of the lot. Sure you'd eat a horse working on the bog, you'd get such an appetite. The tea tasted fantastic – whatever it was, the air maybe.

The tea on the bog was the best of the lot

Tea is central to so many occasions. I went to Dominic St Convent, just up from Parnell St, and after we made our First Holy Communion, we all went back into the convent, and there was a table set out with tea and sandwiches. I remember that so clearly, drinking tea with my mother that day.

I played a lot of hurling and football: that's going back forty years, and tea was part of GAA matches too, particularly championship matches for some reason. At half-time, in the dressing room, everyone would get a cup of tea with two or three spoons of sugar in it – to give you energy. If Dublin were playing a GAA game down the country, I always brought my wife and children down to matches, and we would have the tea and sandwiches out of the boot of the car.

A tea break for firefighters Chris Fox, Declan Egan, Mick Gurley and Gomez Gorman.

COURTESY GER TREHY

I have my own little teapot in the fire station, which was handed down to me by a fella that retired, John Williams. He used the tea leaves, like me, so we'd always have tea together. Night duty is probably the most significant time to have tea for our fire crew. We do twelve-hour shifts, 7 p.m. to 7 a.m. and in our own crew, at about 9.30 p.m. we do something we christened 'story time'. We sit down with our tea and it starts off with 'Do you remember such and such?' and we talk about various incidents that have taken place. Everyone tells stories and one story kicks off another yarn in someone else's mind. There are eight to ten of us around the table, and there's usually a bit of slagging and good craic.

The stories span a thirty-year period and even before that, because I'm thirty-four years in the Airport Police Fire Service and I would have worked with fellas who retired a long time ago, who told me their own stories, so the stories are passed down from generation to generation.

Tea is a social outlet in the workplace. In this job, we have to deal with serious incidents, where there might be a fatality. You don't know what you're going to come up against, day to day. If you have to have a debriefing in the Staff Welfare Office, you are given a cup of tea and you can chat about what's happened. You'd drink the tea whether you wanted it or not. I suppose there is a degree of shock involved as well, but I suppose you deal with it because you've no choice.

I think we drink a lot of tea in Ireland because it's a great Irish tradition for people to call to each other's houses, and the first thing you are offered is a cup of tea. As they say in Offaly, people go 'rambling'.

We all have nicknames in the station. Mine is 'Suede'. Back in the 1970s there were skinheads and 'suede-heads' and I always had my hair short and brushed back. A suede-head was just above a skinhead. Now I was never a suede-head in my life but the same chap that gave me the teapot, John Williams, had a nickname for everyone. He started calling me 'Suede' and there's another fella who works with us, Des Kelly, and he's known as 'Hall, Stairs and Landing' because of Des Kelly Carpets.

ANDREW MALCOLM

Andrew at his
usual whale-
watching
spot on Ram
Head with his
assistant,
Ocho.

COURTESY
ANN TRIMBLE

Andrew Malcolm spends his time carrying out regular watches for the Irish Whale and Dolphin Group (IWDG), and foraging wild plants and mushrooms from the fields and forests and seashore, which he supplies to local restaurants in Wexford. He also builds his own guitars and composes and records music in a converted barn at the foot of the Knockmealdown Mountains, where he lives with his wife, Ann, two horses, seven ducks, a sheep and a dog. It's quite crowded.

The formative years of my life were spent in various towns in Northern Ireland, but the most significant days were spent in the small County Antrim town of Portrush. Here my school friends introduced me to many new delights: Veda bread, soda farls and red lemonade, to name but a few. The foodstuff that really stood out for me though was the Norn Iron special brew known as 'let-it-stand'. Having been brought up by an English mother and a Scottish father this was to prove to be a startling discovery. It all started off very innocently as my mother made me and my recently acquired young friends a pot of tea. She was about to pour when one of them, Niall, said 'Just let it stand for a wee while.' My mother looked a bit nonplussed but, being the perfect hostess, complied with her guest's wishes.

Ten-year-old Niall looked in the teapot and proclaimed, 'We need another two teabags, missus'. These were supplied and Niall put the pot back on the hot plate and proceeded to boil the contents – sacrilege to an English gentlewoman! Five minutes later the brew was declared to be ready and I had my first ever cup of 'let-it-stand'. Initially, the most startling thing was the colour of the tea coming out of the pot. Imagine, if you will, a peat river in full spate and you begin to get a hint of the liquid's dark imaginings. I then watched in astonishment as my friends added four teaspoons of sugar each to their individual mugs. I soon discovered why they were doing this as I took a sip of my non-sweetened tea. Not only was it strong enough to float a bullet but it was also incredibly bitter. So began my addiction to this distinctively Northern Irish delight.

Imagine a peat river in full spate and you begin to get a hint of the liquid's dark imaginings.

My father was a skilful man and made many of his own tools, the most frightening of which was an electric circular saw that he had rigged up as a table saw with a foot switch.

Once, he cut off the top half of his left index finger. Wrapping the stump in a towel to staunch the bleeding he had then spent ten minutes looking for the rest of his finger before thinking that he should go to hospital. He actually got into his car before deciding that it would perhaps be safer if someone else drove him to the emergency ward.

So he walked the couple of hundred yards to our landlord's house. He explained to Joe what had happened and asked him if he would drive him to hospital.

Joe collapsed in shock.

So the supposed patient, my dad, made the supposed saviour, Joe, a nice hot cup of sweet tea and sat with him until he regained his composure. He decided that it was probably going to be counter-productive at this juncture to ask Joe if he would help him look for his lost finger so he settled for a lift to hospital instead.

A fin whale emerges in front of Hook Head Lighthouse.

COURTESY ANDREW MALCOLM

We never did find the missing digit and I still strongly suspect that our dog had gotten to it first. But my father got great mileage out of his half-finger. Whenever you asked him when he'd be ready for his tea, he'd hold up his left index finger for 'half a minute'.

But most of all he got great enjoyment from disgusting and delighting children by pretending to be picking his nose with his finger stuck way up there. The shrieks, when some new kid thought that he'd lost the rest of his finger up his nostril when he withdrew his stump, were priceless.

In 1995 I decided to give up tea, coffee and alcohol for Lent. I haven't drunk a 'proper' cup of tea since and have rarely missed it. Instead I started drinking herbal teas or, as my friend and neighbour John calls them, 'woopsie teas'. This initially manifested itself as exclusively commercially produced infusions, but over the years as I've become more and more involved in foraging I have started producing my own concoctions, with varying degrees of success. The young leaves of brambles and raspberries work well but I have yet to find a cup of tea made from seaweed that I can finish.

All through the year I spend a lot of my free time on the cliff top at Ram Head, Ardmore, being kept warm both by my dog Ocho and a cup of woopsie tea as I look out to sea, watching for the distant 'blows' of whales and the playful splashes of racing dolphins.

IMELDA BYRNE

Imelda Byrne has been a member of the ICA since 1974 and has served as president of Carlow Federation. Imelda is probably best known for her role in RTÉ's reality series *ICA Bootcamp*.

I was born in Limerick, we travelled right around. You name a county and I've lived there. When I was twenty, I joined Aer Lingus and flew from Dublin to New York. We served tea and coffee and meals on the flight and of course we had first class. We also had the 'Golden Shamrock Service' and that's where I developed my taste for caviar. Very few people could afford to travel first class so there was always champagne and caviar left over. You couldn't take the food off the aeroplane because of health restrictions so we always had our fill of caviar. It was only Danish caviar – it wasn't Beluga – but I got quite a taste for it. When Paul and I married, Aer Lingus gave us a free first class flight to New York and we travelled Golden Shamrock with Royal Tara china cups. Everybody else got plastic down the back, but in first class it was Royal Tara.

When I was twenty-eight I stopped flying, and spent four years in America doing PR for Aer Lingus. Americans don't do tea. I used to stay in a hotel and do my stint and then go on to the next place. I was a woman travelling alone in hotels in the 1960s which wasn't looked on especially well. I used to find it uncomfortable going down to the restaurant for breakfast so I got into the habit of ordering breakfast in my room and I'd ring down and say, 'may I have orange juice, tea and toast. Now, please, will you put the tea into the pot and wait until the water is bubbling and then pour it on top', because normally they would bring you a jug of hot water and a teabag in the dish. On one trip, I went up the west coast from San Francisco to Portland to Seattle and over the border into Vancouver. In the hotel there, I made my usual phone call to reception: 'may I have orange juice, tea and toast and would you put the tea in first and the water must be boiling …' and then a very irate voice came back: 'Madam, you are in British territory now, and we do know how to make tea.' I was put in my place, and it was a marvellous cup of tea, it was proper tea.

I was in New York when John F. Kennedy was assassinated and that was extraordinary. Because my plane was in late, I slept late. I knew he had been shot but nobody had said he was dead, just that he had been rushed to hospital. On my way to the Aer Lingus office, which was on Fifth Avenue, when I got up to the news vendors I saw that the President was dead; that was a shock. You could see that everybody was absolutely shocked. There was a huge crowd outside the Aer Lingus building, and when I got up close I saw why. It was an old building with a mezzanine-floor balcony and the window glass came from above that down to the ground and our advertising department had got an enormous portrait of John F. Kennedy looking into the distance, in a plain gold frame. They had hung it out from the mezzanine and the lights were off and somebody had bought a bolt of purple silk and draped it from the floor up over the top of the frame, and just in front was a tall narrow pedestal with an even taller vase holding one Easter lily and one light shining on it. I saw a woman kneel down on the pavement and pray and there were tears and lamentation and it really was heart-rending. I was so proud that Aer Lingus had done that before anyone else.

I was in New York when John F. Kennedy was assassinated and that was extraordinary.

It was great fun working for Aer Lingus and it was sort of glamorous then. There were very few of us and when I went to America I always went with another girl, Josephine McCarthy, who was from Mayo, and Jo and I worked the flight together. We left Dublin at half past ten at night, picked up most of our people in Shannon and then it was eight and a half hours across the Atlantic to Gander, Newfoundland, and then an hour in Gander for breakfast and refuelling, then four and a half hours down to New York, so it was a long saga. Then we got two nights' stay-over in New York, so we had great fun there. I remember Jo and I, on our days off, going down Fifth Avenue and Madison and people staring at us. We sometimes caught hands and girls didn't do that in those days and we wore our miniskirts and we were about eighteen months ahead of girls in New York. The four years I lived in New York were splendid: I was young, I was single, I had a good job, I had a nice apartment. But bringing up a family there would have been difficult. I re-met my husband after twelve years and came home to Ireland to marry him.

My husband and I lived up in the Dublin Mountains before moving to a lovely old Georgian house in County Carlow when our girls were eight and nine years old. I wanted a rural upbringing for my children, where they didn't have to mature too fast.

How I joined the ICA is very simple. I was stuck three miles outside Tullow, with two little girls and a husband who came home only at weekends and in the 1970s women were not invited anywhere without their husbands, so that was lonely. I was repairing an old house and learning how to farm 44 acres, and growing strawberries, and apart from going to the shop and meeting the parents of the other children at the school, I wasn't seeing anyone. Then my neighbour suggested I come down to the local ICA meeting. So I did and I wasn't lonely again. They were lovely women and we met in a little one-room school. We had to sit on top of the desks, we couldn't squeeze into them, but we had such fun there, such camaraderie, just good friendship and such a lot of tea and cakes.

The ICA was started in Bree in County Wexford, in 1910. I think the ICA saved a lot of women from loneliness, because they had very constricted lives then. The ICA only started because they were being taught housewifely skills and their husbands knew where they were, so they were let out and what they did when they were let out, they didn't tell their husbands. But that was the times.

I remember one trip to the Aran Islands by train, with the Bagenalstown guild, twenty-two of us. We got a train to Dublin and then a train to Galway. We had two hours in Galway before the bus that would take us to the port to get the boat to the Aran Islands, so my friend Annette Reddy and I went and saw the Claddagh, the Spanish Arch, St Nicholas' Church where Christopher Columbus prayed before he left for America and Lynch's town castle. We had a cup of tea and then went looking for the others and they weren't at the bus stop. We had to go on a search for them. We found all of them in Dunnes Stores. They were let loose in Galway and they went to Dunnes.

We got there eventually and the Aran Islands were marvellous; we really had a lovely time. On the way back, the Galway train was a little late and we thought we would miss the last train to Carlow. We told the ticket collector and he phoned ahead and when we got to Dublin, they were waiting for us. They said 'run', so we all had to run. Imagine twenty-two women galloping from one platform to the other. That was a bit of an adventure.

The ICA has been a big part of my life. At our monthly meetings in the parish hall, we always have a cup of tea. One lady in the guild is asked to bring sandwiches and one is asked to bring cakes, so they are the two hostesses for the night, and it alternates, nobody has to do it too often. We have had speakers from the fire service, the ambulance service, Red Cross, the VEC, a physiotherapist, a lawyer, or speakers on fun subjects like drama, make-up and crafts. We also teach one another our crafts or skills. It is a get-together, the cup of tea and a chat, that's the business.

I like good old-fashioned 'trot a mouse' Barry's tea. For convenience I use teabags, but I do like it from a teapot, and I just can't drink my tea out of a mug. Although I did have to adapt somewhat in recent years. Paul, my husband, had Parkinson's and was quite shaky and he couldn't manage a cup and saucer, and a mug was too heavy, so I had special mugs handmade by a man called John Cummins in Bagenalstown. They are nice and light. It made it so comfortable for Paul. He could hold it, and he could slide it onto the saucer and it was marvellous. I had a dozen of them, and as a matter of fact I have given away most of them when I meet people with the same problem.

In the 1950s when I first joined Aer Lingus, I had a flat with one of the girls who flew with me, Ursula Crotty. Sometimes, if we got a day off together, we would say 'let's do a bit of gracious living', so we would take our time and get all gussied up in our best gear and go down to the Shelbourne for afternoon tea. That was the epitome of gracious living – afternoon tea in the Shelbourne. We took a stroll through Grafton Street, came out through Brown Thomas and finished up at the Shelbourne for afternoon tea. It was wonderful.

Afternoon tea at the Shelbourne Hotel, Dublin.

I feel great and at this stage of my life I am a member of 'Older and Bolder'. I am not 'elderly' – such a condescending word. I am older and that's it. There's a great freedom about being older and not having to conform and being allowed to be yourself at last.

Who would have thought I would become a television star at seventy-nine! But taking part in the four series of *ICA Bootcamp* really has been a great experience. You know, people still come up and ask for photographs with you. But sometimes men come up and ask, 'are you the lady from ICA Bootcamp?' And you say yes, and then they burst out laughing. That wasn't exactly the impression I wanted to make on men, but there you are.

ANNE BROLLY

Anne Brolly is a well-known singer/songwriter and politician from County Derry. Anne's son Joe is a former Derry Gaelic footballer and television pundit.

When we were children, we had a range in our kitchen and the kettle was never off the boil. My mother poured tea all day long. One old lady who used to come to our house would read your tea leaves for you. They used to call her 'Mary Forty Bags' because she used to boil the big bags of flour and sew them up to be used as sheets. She would say, 'now, you're getting a letter from America' and 'you're going on a journey' or 'there's a tall dark stranger in there', especially when we were going to the dances. The only time she wouldn't tell your fortune was during Lent; she used to say the priest didn't allow her to read the cups during Lent. Of course, because we were young, we believed everything she told us.

I remember, too, if you were visiting somebody's house and you said, 'oh no, I'll not take any tae,' they would say 'ach, you'll take a drop in your hand,' and that meant you didn't have to eat anything and they didn't have to sit you at the table. If you ran out of tea, you would be sent next door for some; the saying was 'go and ask Mary to give you a wee lock of tae.'

When I was only a child, my mother used to talk about people dyeing their hair with tea – they would put the comb in black tea and comb it through their hair every morning, because there wouldn't have been hair colouring then. Both women and men probably did it. I remember one woman who did it. There were parts of her hair brown and parts of it a mahogany colour, and people would say, 'ah sure, she always puts the cold tae through her hair.'

I like tea, as they say here, 'brave and strong'. I don't like weak tea. I remember we had an American visitor in the house one day and I asked him, 'how do you like your tea? Would you like it weak or strong?' And he looked at the teapot and said to me, 'how would you do that?' We all know you give the person who takes weak tea the first cup and the person who takes strong tea the last cup, or you stir the pot, but he didn't know that. So I said 'well, what you do is you say the magic word before you pour.'

I like tea, as they say here, 'brave and strong'

In rural Ireland years ago, tea was often drunk out of a bowl, what they called the 'babhal' of tea. They had cups but preferred a bowl. A country man wouldn't thank you for a teacup; it wouldn't hold near enough tea, for a start.

Tea is therapeutic, of course – to sit down and have a cup of tea, especially when you get bad news. Tea is so much a part of everything we do, even in the GAA. We always brought a picnic and a flask to GAA matches. There was always tea after training sessions, too. The GAA halls were the great community hub and there was always tea and sandwiches after GAA functions.

When I started to sing at about nine years old, we had a group in Coalisland where I lived. I remember going to sing in Bellaghy on a Sunday. We thought that was great to get in a car and get away all day. You would get up and get your hair done and you were going to sing in the concert. The man who organised it used always say, 'well, you know, you won't be getting anything for it but you'll get your tea.' We thought this was great because that meant you would get your tea and you would get wee buns and nice sandwiches – you wouldn't get any fancy buns at home.

When we started our local Comhaltas Ceoltóirí Éireann branch, we would go to the different houses and there would be a session and they would always have tea. If you weren't offered any, you would have said 'that's a cold house there; they didn't even offer us a cup of tea.'

Years ago, people were always in and out of each other's houses, not like nowadays, and the kettle was always ready on the hob. My husband Francie's grandmother had a great wee saying. When someone came into the house, someone in the family would say to them, 'will you take a cup of tea?' but his granny would say, 'Put on the kettle. "Willyou" is a bad friend.'

Tea very often would have been seen as an alternative to alcohol. There was an old saying, 'tea is the cup that cheers but does not inebriate.' There was another saying in the olden days, before teabags, when someone didn't put much tea in the teapot, they would say 'That's Shamrock tea', meaning it was made with just three leaves.

Refreshments at a dinner dance, 1940s.
COURTESY INDEPENDENT NEWSPAPERS IRELAND

PETER KELLY

Peter Kelly's company Weddings by Franc is Ireland's leading wedding planning and event design company, and Peter has filmed over thirty television programmes for his RTÉ series *Brides of Franc, Engagement with Franc* and *Franc's DIY Brides.*

Peter Kelly in his tea rooms at Glanworth Mill, Cork. COURTESY AMY CRONIN

I prefer to drink tea from a china cup but I am happy to drink from whatever is offered. In our tea rooms at Glanworth Mill, we love to use vintage china cups. Tea rooms are going through a big revival at the moment. They used to be a common gathering place years ago and now they're coming back into fashion. I think it has a lot to do with fashion, because everyone is looking back to the 1920s, 1930s and 1950s. The

TV drama series *Downton Abbey* also has a lot to answer for – it showed the ritual of tea drinking and afternoon tea and has probably revived the whole industry.

When we designed the tea rooms at Glanworth Mill, I wanted to create a vintage feel and serve tea and coffee in china cups and give it an olde worlde charm because the mill is such an old building, dating back to the eighteenth century.

I like the ritual of making tea. I like Barry's tea, probably because I grew up with it in west Cork. I like iced fruit teas probably because I spent happy days working in the Caribbean as a young chef. Mint tea is nice but it always reminds me of a diet. I drink strong tea: if I'm drinking Barry's loose tea I will add a pinch of Darjeeling to give it a little kick.

I like the ritual of making tea.

I'm very fussy about teapots. There are very few good pouring teapots. Most of them dribble when you pour, and that drives me mad. You often see people with a little scrunchie around the base of the spout to catch the drips.

My father was born in Galway and my mother was born in Edinburgh. We lived in England until I was seven and the kettle was always on the boil. My Irish grandmother also lived with us. She made lovely brown bread, soda bread and loved a cup of tea. My first experience with tea was with my dad and Grandma Kelly.

We moved to west Cork in 1976. Cork is home now but it was a big culture shock when I first moved there. I came from a large city school with a thousand students to a beautiful little school called Clogagh National School in west Cork with only about 100 pupils, and a building that still had open fires in the classrooms. There were only two in my class – me and a little girl called Martina.

The boys sat on one side and the girls sat on the other, but I sat at the same little desk as Martina because there were only the two of us in our class, so I was the only one who shared a desk with a girl. I think that's why I became very in tune with the female of the species. It started at a very early age!

I remember on my first day, suddenly all the other kids got up and reached into their satchels and brought out glass bottles filled with tea, stuffed at the top with a twist of newspaper. They brought all the glass bottles up and stood them next to the open fire. I asked a boy, 'what are you all doing?' He said, 'We're bringing up the tea'. So I brought up my flask, with Mickey Mouse on the side, and placed it with the rest of them. Of course, later on, when we went to get our tea, I discovered my flask was completely melted. But they all now had hot tea. I had never seen tea in a bottle, with a twist of newspaper as a stopper, until I came to west Cork. That was 1976, but it sounds like 1926.

In third class we had to make tea for the teachers. I thought that was terrible. I had come from a school where we had school dinners made for us. Teddy was a big guy in the class and we became friends. I remember him telling me, 'Kelly, we have to go and make tea'. And I said, 'what?' 'We have to make tea for the teachers, boy,' he said. I was shocked. Had they not heard of health and safety?

I said, 'This is slave labour Teddy.' He said, 'No, no it's not. We all take turns.' I said, 'I guarantee after today we'll never have to make tea again.' He said, 'Are you sure?' and I said 'Teddy, I guarantee you, me and you will never have to make tea again.'

So I washed the teapot really well with soap, made the tea, and left it on the fire for the teachers. At the first break, eleven o'clock, the tea was about ready. We were sent out, as usual, in the freezing cold to the bicycle shed, and the teachers were inside having their tea in front of the lovely fire. But Teddy and I watched through the window and saw them literally spit the tea out across the table. We never had to make the tea again after that.

I had a fantastic time in Clogagh National School. I have really happy memories and feel lucky to have been brought up in west Cork, a place I love so much.

RÓISÍN O

Róisín O is a singer-songwriter who has shared stage and studio with some of Ireland's leading artists. www.RoisinO.com

When we recorded 'Tea Song' we needed a video. Our band have so many friends and relatives who have had to emigrate to study or for work, we thought this would be a great excuse to get back in touch with them, and do something with them for the video for 'Tea Song', and then we realised there are probably fans abroad who might be interested, too, so we put out the word through Facebook, our website and Twitter, and we got a huge response. People from all over the world sent us videos of them drinking tea, often in exotic locations, on busy city streets or even in the ocean. Each person told us how long they had been away from Ireland, and we decided to write the number of days they have been away at the bottom of the screen.

Brian Murphy, my bass player, wrote the song and I think it's about waking up the morning after a night out and not feeling very good, and just drinking pots and pots of tea to make yourself feel better – there's something comforting about tea. Brian is a great songwriter.

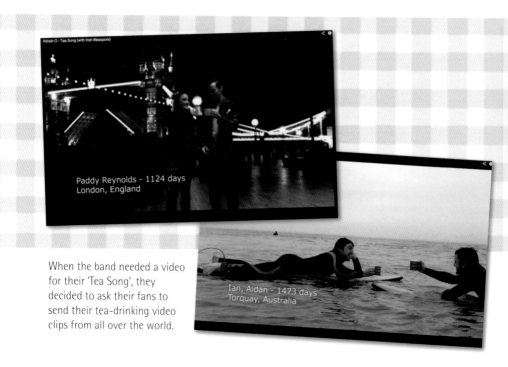

Paddy Reynolds - 1124 days
London, England

Ian, Aidan - 1473 days
Torquay, Australia

When the band needed a video for their 'Tea Song', they decided to ask their fans to send their tea-drinking video clips from all over the world.

Actually, he takes his tea so strong, no wonder he wrote a song about tea! I couldn't drink it. He stands by the kettle for ages, just squeezing the teabag.

I love my tea. I didn't start drinking tea until I was about seventeen, which was quite old for my family. I have two older brothers and they started drinking tea when they were about nine. I remember my brother Danny saying, 'Róisín, you just have to try it. You have to drink tea.' I tried it with sugar, and Danny was appalled at this. But our whole family are real tea drinkers now. The kettle is constantly on. And we all take it the same way: Barry's, strong, with a little milk, and no sugar. I've also started drinking more tea lately. It used to be about two a day, now it's with every meal and maybe one in between meals with a biscuit. We always bring teabags abroad with us, too. But Irish milk is so good, when you bring Barry's tea abroad, the different milk and water can mean you don't get a proper cup. You have to have all the ingredients right.

Greg Purcell - 76 days
New York, USA

David White - 800 days
Kyoto, Japan

I lived in San José, California, for a year and the tea over there is really, really bad so I brought loads of Barry's teabags to sustain me. In November, I went on tour with my mam and we forgot to bring teabags and it was the worst thing ever. At the end of the tour we visited my uncle who lives in San Francisco and he had a big hoard of Barry's, so when we got there it was 'yeah, tea, at last.'

My mam and I go on a folk cruise every year, where I sing with the Black family, and it's a great cruise. It's all folk and Irish music, and all the musicians are either Irish or of Irish heritage. These cruise ships are massive, and everyone sits down to this big dinner and the Irish are all in one section, and they organise a walk-around with a box of Barry's teabags after dinner. We also try to explain to the waiters that we need boiling, bubbling water, not just hot water. It's the only way to make good tea.

I suppose the Irish love of tea stems from how our parents and their parents just always drank tea. My grandparents didn't have a TV so in the evening, sitting around and having a cup of tea and a biscuit and a chat was their entertainment. And, of course, it's hot, and that helps in Ireland where it's so cold.

Myself and my friends all love tea. We often hang out and drink tea all night, pot after pot. I like big mugs, I'm greedy about my tea!

EAMON DALLETT

Eamon Dallett has worked in the Civil Service since 1970 and lives in Dungiven, County Derry.

It's amazing when you think about the impact tea has had on Irish people. I first became aware of the importance of tea when I was about eight. We lived in the country, in Kilrea, close to the River Bann and a few miles from the Sperrins, in County Derry. The first really positive thing about tea that I can remember was that it covered the taste of goat's milk. Like many poor people at that time throughout Ireland, our milk supply came from our goat and goat's milk has a strong herbal taste due to the herbs and leaves on which the goat feeds. As a young boy I plainly recollect I didn't like it, but I discovered it was handy enough in tea. There were no milkmen calling to houses back then.

I remember one great use for the tea chest was for rearing pet pigs. A pet pig was the baby that was rejected by the sow, a wee small effort that had to be fed by bottle and it was put in a tea chest beside the range for a few weeks. The tea chest was an absolutely ideal home for it.

Another great association I have with tea is turf cutting. We heated our house by burning turf then. A lot of turf cutting used to go on nearby at Drumimerick just outside Kilrea and tea is such a big thing on 'the moss' (as we call the bog in Derry). We cycled the two or three miles to the moss but we took with us bottles of tae and it was milked and all. One of the funny things about that tea was I remember getting it cool and enjoying it, but you would only ever drink cool tea in the moss. Because the bog is very, very cool, to keep the tea cool we would bury the bottles until lunchtime. Of course, at home if tea got very cool, I couldn't drink it.

On the moss, all across the country, people drank the tea out of little mugs that were soldered together by the Travellers. You wouldn't have taken delph or china to the bog so those tin mugs were standard issue.

Tea is also very important when it allows people to talk. There are a lot of lonely people today. I come across lots of stories like that through my involvement with the local St Vincent de Paul. The deprivation and difficulty out there at the moment is nothing ordinary. I used to think that the state social services would cope with most problems, but now I have learned that that is not the case. There is a lot of suffering.

I also think it's a disadvantage socially if you don't drink tea, because it opens the door to conversation. I would equate it to smoking a few years ago. I

It's a disadvantage socially if you don't drink tea

remember in a work situation, a good number of my colleagues smoked and would have gone along to a smokers' room and the smokers were the best-informed people about what was going on and they enjoyed that. The tea can be a similar sort of thing.

I remember my wife Mary's father, Kevin, telling me about drinking tea from china cups and holding your little finger aloft. It was seen as posh. It was the first time I ever realised there was a kind of social status about drinking out of china cups. If we were having tea somewhere, when we came home, Kevin would ask us: 'had you the wee finger out?'

We tend to drink Twinings tea nowadays. Twinings to Mary and me would be sort of the Rolls Royce of tea. I drink on average seven cups a day, but depending on the situation it could be more than that, seldom fewer.

My daughter Roisín lives in Kildare with her family, and when we visit them we do drink Lyons or Barry's because we know it's good, too. She knows we love tea. Roisín wouldn't go for a cheap brand of tea anyway. We tried to raise her with standards!

Roisín doesn't know that we sometimes sneak the wains wee sups of tea, but what she doesn't know won't harm her. They don't give their children tea, but it gives us great pleasure, Mary and I, if we can slip the child a wee sup of tea. And they love it, especially wee Oisín, who is two. He comes to my wife and says, 'Tea, Granny Mary?' Associating the tea with us, Granny and Granddad – that makes it all the more satisfying for us, too.

Lily Mae Lane enjoys tea parties. Every Saturday morning she comes into her parents Peter and Mary's bedroom with her Winnie-the-Pooh tea set and offers them 'tup-a-tae'. It's never too early for a tea party.

JOE DONNELLY AND KEITH WALSH

Joe (left) and Keith present the breakfast show on Dublin rock station Phantom 105.2.

How do you take your tea?

Keith: I love a strong cup of tea, or 'a cup of tar', as me granny would have called it, with a small drop of milk and no sugar. Although I don't like it as strong as my wife's granny, who always had the tea 'on the go' on the 'range'. Her tea would stew all day and every now and then she'd add another spoon of tea or a drop of boiling water from the kettle (also boiling all day on the range). That tea was horrible, that tea was also used when the tractor ran out of diesel.

Joe: If tea isn't really strong then it's not tea; it's a sick joke not to serve powerfully strong tea. The process of making tea, from the growth and harvesting of a plant to the bag you put in your cup deserves more respect than a milky-pale end result.

If tea isn't really strong then it's not tea

How many cups per day?

Keith: Depends on the day but if it's a working day it could be up to ten cups. Because I present a breakfast radio show I'm up very early and before I've even opened my eyes I'm downstairs putting the kettle on and if I have time I'll bring tea in my flask for the train. I'll then switch to coffee for the day and then back to the tea when I get home.

Joe: Two or three in the evening time. I look forward to the cups of tea as much as my dinner. In fact, certain dinners are greatly complemented by a cup of tea. Some people say that having a cup of tea with your dinner – as opposed to afterwards – is a real 'country' thing to do. They say it's only the farmer who has his dinner at noon that would engage in this practice. Regardless of the origins of having tea with the dinner, or whether it's part of the urban-rural divide, I won't stop having a hot mug of strong tea sitting next to my meal. However, it would only be with ordinary meat-and-two-veg dinners, or maybe a spaghetti Bolognese if I was feeling adventurous. A curry or a stir-fry is not complemented by a mug of tea.

Do you have a favourite brand?

Keith: It has to be Lyons: my family have always been a Lyons family. My wife came from a Barry's house but I make her buy Lyons. It was part of our pre-marriage agreement.

Joe: Barry's. I think it's very easy to tell the difference between cheaper and more expensive tea brands and blends. I have no time for herbal teas or flavoured teas.

When did you start drinking tea?

Keith: From a very young age. I used to take it with sugar but then I gave up sugar in my tea for Lent one year and never went back to the sugary tea.

Joe: I don't recall drinking tea as a child. I think I took to it more in my teens. This may have been a result of spending a lot of time – when I should have been studying or in school – in cafés and fast-food outlets. We'd order a pot of tea and nineteen cups and spend an afternoon talking absolute garbage to each other and wondering why we couldn't get a girlfriend.

Any memorable tea moments?

Keith: One of my earliest memories involves tea drinking. I must have been only about seven and there was some building going on in my estate. I started chatting to the builders. I would call into them on the site when they were having their tea, and one of them would give me a cup of tea out of his flask. This went on until the end of the summer holidays and it always makes me smile when I think about it. It would never happen these days, which in one way is sad but in another way is probably right.

Joe: I must have been six or seven years old and my gran gave myself and my older brother the mugs with the chocolate eggs in them one Easter. Mine was a Manchester United mug, his was Liverpool. I didn't know anything about football at the time, but when Phil wanted to swap with my mug I knew there must have been a good reason for it, so I hung on tight. And so began my dedication to Manchester United. Younger people won't remember the pain of being a United supporter in the 1980s so it's nice that they've done so well over the past, I don't know, two decades it must be now, is it?

Why is it, do you think, that Irish people love tea so much?

Keith: It's the comfort of a warm drink. It's not too expensive so it's a cheap treat, also the Irish are awkward with other people so as soon as you arrive at a friend's house you'll be offered a cup of tea. This will give the host something to do until the initial awkwardness dissipates.

Joe: Tea and chatting or storytelling go hand-in-hand and the Irish are well known for their love of talking and telling tales. We're a hospitable race and serving tea is probably the simplest gesture that any host, regardless of their age or background, can make. You might be on your uppers but you'll surely be able to offer a visitor a cup of tea. Historically, we probably picked up the habit from our neighbours across the water; it wouldn't surprise me if they got us addicted to tea in order to keep us distracted with all the chatting and storytelling.

LEANORA O'HALLORAN

Leanora O'Halloran, from Oughterard, County Galway, is a Support Officer for Community Arts in Clann Family Resource Centre.

COURTESY LEANORA O'HALLORAN

I love tea. I have done ever since I had my first sip at the young age of three – I have the picture to prove it. Ever since then we've had a flawless relationship – always there to warm me up when cold, relax me when stressed, and to comfort me when times are not so good. There's nothing quite like coming home after being away and having the first sip of hot tea. The words just spill out: 'ah ... that's a lovely cup of tea'.

I'm positive tea has magical properties: once people get a mug of tea in their hands it's almost like an invisible barrier breaks down and people feel free to set loose all their worries, anxieties and fears. It's amazing the deep conversations that can come out of sharing the experience of drinking a cup of tea with somebody ... that said, many a ridiculous conversation has been had in my house over cups of tea, especially if it's during the cup of tea that has to be had after a night out, which, of course, calls for not just tea, but tea and toast.

I work in a Family Resource Centre and it's remarkable how important a cup of tea is to the people who come into the centre; many times I have been told that it is the cup of tea before the class that really gives people the therapy they need, the freedom to talk to the other people in the group, exchanging stories, trials and tribulations – it's therapeutic.

I would drink tea till it came out my ears, one cup after another – I'm sure I get through ten a day. Many a debate is brewed over tea. There is the inevitable statement that 'you can't drink a cup of tea on its own, you have to have something with it', but not to me. To me, all you need is tea.

To me, all you need is tea.

My dad never was one for cooking or cleaning. He was what I suppose you would call an old-style man. If he was at home all day on his own while Mam was out, you could be sure he'd be starving by the time she'd get home. However, once the nine o'clock news was over, you'd be guaranteed he'd make a pot of tea. My dad passed away a few months ago. That cup of tea after the news will never be the same. But it's fitting that now, whenever I make a cup of tea, I see his picture on the kitchen window sill looking back at me – I reminisce about the many cups of tea and chats we once shared – and then his voice pops into my head: 'make sure that's drawn before you pour it!'

GER O'BRIEN

Ger O'Brien studied Zoology at Trinity College Dublin in the mid-1990s and undertook a Masters in Landscape Architecture at Edinburgh College of Art. He graduated in 2001 and has stayed in Scotland since, now practising in Dundee. Outside work, Ger is an artist, exhibiting locally for the past number of years.

COURTESY THERESA LYNN

Hot, hot water, poured over teabag, and most importantly teabag left in the teacup for the duration of the cup. I have some milk in, but no sugar. I gave up sugar in my tea one Lent back in my Catholic days (what a great thing Lent is, when you think about it. Bring back Lent, I say).

Although I love hot, hot water to make the tea, I have no problem with a cold cup of tea, which is normally what I get by the end of the cup. I still relish the cold tea. I have even been known to drink a cup of tea that was left from breakfast half-finished.

Barry's Gold Blend is a wonder, though over here in Scotland I go for Tetley. I had a boyfriend from Taiwan who had lived in Ireland and he was able to get Bewley's loose tea from a wee town near Dundee. I once made the tea for him but put in way too much loose tea, having forgotten what to do with the stuff. To make it palatable we added about a litre of water and were left with oceans of tea, the cups of which sat along the counter for a few days. He refused to throw it out and kept reheating it, so precious was the Bewley's tea to him.

When I worked in America for a summer, in my uni days, my sister sent me a parcel of Irish tea. The Americans couldn't understand my wonder at this parcel, but we Irish know a proper cup of tea is a cup of Irish tea.

My best cups of tea are always experienced outdoors. I used to be quite into walking hills and the best companion on such trips is a flask of tea. Last year I took part in monthly 'mindful' walks. On these short walks, a group of us walked in silence, until one of us called for a drawing to be done which could be any form and some people took this to mean looking around. At the halfway point we would stop and chat, and I always relished my swigs of tea from the flask. You can't take coffee on such walks: it's never as refreshing and it loses its taste. Tea's the thing, especially on a cold day walking.

Tea's the thing, especially on a cold day walking

My partner Louie grew up in Hong Kong and he tells of an unusual use for tea. When he accompanied his family to dinner in a restaurant, green tea was always served. As soon as the tea arrived, his mother proceeded to wash all the cutlery and dishes in the tea water. She believed the hygiene of the restaurant couldn't be guaranteed so she went to work on her cleaning!

I have a favourite mug. I spent £10 on my mug. It's one of a Pantone range. Now, if you are a designer of any kind, you will know about Pantones. Pantones are a specification scheme of colours. My Pantone is number 585, a light green. Pantone pens used to be an essential part of any design. These pens gave flat, beautiful colours to drawings. By the way, colouring in with Pantones or any type of colouring-in implement is referred to as rendering, which I always like to say. I think

Pantone
585

my Pantone colour is very Ger. It is a bright colour, not too serious but friendly. The cup itself is of nice china, so it is quite thin, and rests beautifully on your lower lips.

My best memories of my tea-drinking days are of my friends in our uni days. We were very close and probably very loud back then. There were often plans for study days or evenings round at a friend's flat. Needless to say not a bit of studying was done. As soon as we got through the door the kettle was on and the pot of steaming hot tea was never ending. I don't even think there was much in the way of eating at the time, just a bottomless cup of tea. Our conversations often referred to us trying to understand ourselves, trying to get to the bottom of what we were and how things were, all these musings were added to and washed down by tea. This serious investigation was interspersed with a great deal of laughter.

A tea break while saving hay in the Glen of Aherlow, Tipperary, c. 1925. Back row (l–r): Joan Ryan (later Keith), Mary Kennedy, Nora O'Reilly (née O'Neill) and Ellen Kennedy; front row (l–r): three Kennedy brothers, including William Kennedy (centre), husband of Mary Kennedy. COURTESY TONY AND MARY WALSH

MATT JORDAN

Matt Jordan is an electrical engineer from Dublin. His teapot treasure trove in County Roscommon currently holds over 500 teapots.

I started collecting teapots seven years ago. My mam was doing up her house and she gave me a dresser with three teapots on it, and that started me off. I just added to the collection. Now, when I'm in a shop or at a market, I buy a teapot I like, but I also buy a teapot I don't like, and all the ones in between: I'll buy them as well.

When my partner Breda and I travel, we always bring back a teapot, and friends and family pick them up for us, too. I've bought teapots in markets in Switzerland, Spain and Italy. My sister brought me one from China. A friend from Derry gave me one shaped like the Queen Vic pub in *Eastenders*, and I have a Rovers Return teapot, like the pub in *Coronation Street*. My son's girlfriend brought me one from America, and my son even painted a teapot for my birthday a few years ago. My sister's children like to bring me small toy teapots they buy in a euro shop, with miniature animals inside. The collection is up to well over 500 teapots now.

Breda doesn't even drink tea, but she's happy to go along with it. I've no plans to stop collecting. Sometimes a friend and I discuss what we will do with the teapots. The latest plan was a teapot museum in the shape of a giant teapot! It would be lovely to have them on display for people to come in and see them, and maybe offer tea and a cake.

The most I ever spent was fifty quid. I usually buy them in charity shops because I like that the money goes to charity. Or sometimes if I like a teapot in a restaurant, I ask them to sell it to me. If you see a teapot in an antique shop, you know that someone has bought and used that teapot: I like to think it has a story.

Each year I go to Spain with the lads to play golf, and when we have a day off, we go to a place called Ronda, up in the mountains, and there's a little antique shop there. There's always this old couple sitting at the back of the shop, and they're always fast asleep. They don't even lift their heads when you go in. You have to whisper 'excuse me, can I buy this teapot?' They're in their eighties and opening the shop is probably their excuse to get up in the mornings. I've been going there five or six years, and every time I go there, they're asleep.

If I dropped one or lost one of my teapots tomorrow it wouldn't

bother me, because I haven't got an affection for a particular teapot: it's a collection. If you were to worry about them, you wouldn't sleep. You'd get paranoid and you'd lock them all in a room, but they should be seen, so I don't worry about them.

My grandmother worked in Dublin Zoo as a cook, and my mam worked up there too and later in canteens and office restaurants, so tea was always there. When I left school first, I worked in the zoo, cleaning tables in the restaurant, and I remember the chimpanzee tea parties every Saturday. They'd have the tables laid out on the grass and then they'd bring out the chimps. They always used the babies, before they became too big and aggressive.

I love tea. I'd drink eight or nine cups before ten o'clock some mornings. But actually for years in this house we didn't even have a teapot – and Breda was embarrassed that we had hundreds of teapots on the walls, but we didn't have a teapot we could use to make tea. We made tea in mugs! So we have a metal teapot now for everyday use.

We bring teabags abroad with us because the tea is usually horrible. I find if you're away anywhere in the world, the best place to get a cup of tea is McDonalds, because the McDonalds tea is the same in Copenhagen or Prague or Madrid or Dublin.

I don't like weak tea, but I don't like stewed tea either. I always use a big mug or else I would drink a whole pot. I might go out to the garden and I'd leave my mug and say to Breda, 'don't throw that out', I'd just stick it in the microwave when I come back in. Breda might not drink tea but she's very good for making tea for me. When I first met Breda, she wouldn't have a teabag in the house, now she's surrounded by teapots.

Matt and his partner, Breda.

ERIC KEMP

Eric Kemp hails from Celbridge, County Kildare, and is an archaeologist, accomplished artist, musician and captain of the *Nieuwe Zorgen*.

I remember the first time I stood on a sailing ship. I found myself stuck in Brest, in France, so I went to the local Irish bar hoping the barman would be Irish. Thankfully he was and when he heard my story, he agreed to give me a job and a room. On the second night, in walked three Irish guys who were sailing a Galway hooker and they were short a crew member, so I blagged my way into their crew. The second I stood on that boat, I fell in love. As we sailed out of Brest, I thought 'I'm home, this is what I want to do.' I wanted to get a working boat but, with my disability, I can't go down the official paths to sail. Had I not been sick I'd be in the Merchant Navy, simple as. So the only way was to become a captain myself and get my own boat.

I spent a lot of time in hospital as a child so probably had my first cup of tea in hospital. I remember tea and toast being the only edible thing there. I had cancer. I was in a hospice at five years of age and I

The *Nieuwe Zorgen*, a Dutch skutsje built in 1904, operated out of Akkrum in Friesland until Eric brought her to Ireland in 2007. A glorious sight is to watch a skutsje approaching a bridge with mast and sails up; the skipper pulls on the topping lift, the mast swings down, the boat glides under the bridge, the topping lift is released, the mast swings back up and the boat sails on. COURTESY ERIC KEMP

was the only one to walk out of it. They have no medical explanation for it. At one stage I had a tumour that filled my whole stomach and they cut me open but it was wrapped around all my internal organs, so that was it, they couldn't remove it. They sent me to the hospice and

Mark Reilly (left) with Eric, dressed as pirates for a charity event, and their dogs, Shadow Ten Bears and little Oíche. COURTESY DAVID CONN

told my parents I had five weeks to live. In fact, they told my parents they should go and have another child. My sister Aiveen was born the following year, but over thirty years later I'm still here.

The problem is the damage done by all the medical treatment. The radiation and chemotherapy stunted my growth and most of my internal organs – basically my torso was whacked with radiation. It was a lot to deal with in my teens and drove me a bit mad, but you get over it. Later I went back to the hospital to look at the records, trying to figure it out. Most of the doctors and nurses who had worked on me had died, of cancer, actually. All I found was a note on my file saying that the tumour 'went away'. Recently, an A&E doctor was looking through my records and he said, 'you survived that? That's a miracle.' I said, 'I don't really believe in miracles, what about you?', expecting the same answer, but he said, 'I see them every day. Some people walk out of here who shouldn't.'

On a boat, there's always a cup of tea on the go, and tea is essential when we're moving, because it's so cold out there. When you're hanging

off the tiller and the rain is beating down and someone hands you a cup of tea, it's so welcome. The enamel cups also double as hot water bottles.

My boat is a sailing boat, 60 feet long, called *Nieuwe Zorgen*, and she's 108 years old. She was originally a Dutch cargo vessel. She was sunk in the Second World War so the Nazis couldn't get her. You generally don't see sailing boats on canals because there aren't many that can drop the mast and sail under bridges. Also, the flat design of this hull enables us to go places a lot of other boats can't. We've even crossed the canal over the M50. That was some sight! I'd love to charter the boat but my disability means I wouldn't pass the insurance medicals, so I developed the idea of sailing for charity. Over the last few years we've been working for a charity that helps people with disabilities.

I was given strict tea instructions when I was younger that the water has to be boiling and you never boil the water twice. I'm currently instructing several French friends about the importance of boiling water versus tepid water. I take sugar and milk in my tea. People have tried to get me onto hippy teas and all sorts of strange teas but it's not the same without milk and sugar.

My favourite tea blend is Earl Grey. I usually drink two cups of tea in the morning before it kicks in. I drink at least ten cups a day. I don't drink alcohol and I play music with a lot of friends who don't drink either, so when we play in pubs we drink tea. On those nights you could drink ten cups of tea in the one evening. Years ago, I used to sing in a metal band, but hadn't the foggiest what I was doing. In a later life, I got back into it again and now I play low whistle, guitar and mandolin.

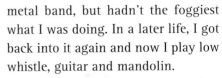

There is a strong connection between tall ships and tea.

There is a strong connection between tall ships and tea. The tea clippers were huge sailing ships, the biggest ever built, and the 1800s saw an annual race around the world to get the tea back to the London market. It was a serious business to make the first delivery and get the best price. They would battle their way through storms, through the most dangerous waters on the planet, risking their lives, just to get this tea back to London.

When I travel I bring teabags, but when I visit my French girlfriend it's not a problem, because you can get Twinings Earl Grey in France. When we were younger, we cycled a lot through Europe, and the tea in the evening was the best part of the day. The fire was lit and the tents were up. We didn't have a teapot so it was just a pot, and we had to reuse the teabags because we were quite poor. But the joy it brought us. I could survive anything, but not without my tea.

With our little tribe on the canal, when anyone calls to us, the first thing you do is put on the kettle. According to ancient laws of hospitality, you fed and watered a guest without saying a word to them – not a word until they were full. There were practical reasons for that, too: if someone was coming to your tribe to kill you, he'd be less likely to harm you if he had a full belly and was feeling happy about himself.

I love sailing. Being sick taught me one very important lesson – don't waste your time doing stuff you don't want to do.

THE EVOLUTION OF THE TEABAG

In the 1900s, a New York tea merchant called Thomas Sullivan wanted to send some samples to his customers so he packed small amounts of his tea leaves in little bags made from silk. On receiving these 'teabags' in the post, some of Sullivan's customers assumed they were similar to the metal infusers that were popular at the time and put the entire bag in their teapot instead of emptying out the tea leaves. They later suggested to Sullivan that the silk bags should be more porous so he developed gauze sachets.
The teabag was born.

ALPS WOMEN'S GROUP

ALPS Women's Group in Trim, County Meath, pictured with some of their prized teapots, tea caddies and delph.

BRIGID MADDEN

Our local women's group, 'ALPS', started here in Trim in 1991. There was a lot of unemployment at that time, like today, so the VEC and Trim Forum organised a meeting down in the town hall and we formed the Adult Learning Programme. There was a series of talks by guest speakers for so many weeks, and men came in the beginning but they were greatly outnumbered and it evolved into the women's group we

Above: Cora Byrne (left) and Brigid with their 'teabag tablecloth'.

Right: Brigid with one of her handmade tea cosies.

have today. When we started, we used to have a childcare facility, but most of us are past needing that now.

We meet every Tuesday morning and, of course, the cup of tea is the centre of the morning, and other activities often result from discussions over tea. Some of the members go to exercise classes and we also run short courses – in crafts, jewellery making and computers – and we invite speakers along. Nowadays, we like to say that ALPS stands for Adult Learning and Leisure Programme. Our emphasis today is more on leisure. A lot of people who wouldn't do certain things on their own will do so as part of a group. We all know each other so well now, too. When I was ill a few years ago, and my mother and brother died, the group provided so much support. You can shed tears here and no one will judge you.

We decided to make our 'teabag tablecloth' to mark our twentieth anniversary. We saw it as a symbol of all the people who have been part of ALPS over the years and all the cups of tea we have enjoyed together. We emptied out teabags and then glued them in sections to form the tablecloth. We dyed some to make the flower designs. By cutting the round teabags in half we formed the scalloped edge around the tablecloth. There are about 1,200 teabags in the final piece. We kept all the tea leaves we removed in a vase.

I love tea, although there were a few times in my life when I couldn't drink it: every time I was pregnant, I went off the tea and sipped 7Up instead. After the first baby, I knew that if I went off the tea that was it, I was pregnant – I didn't even need to go to the doctor for a test.

When we were going to school we brought our tea in an empty sauce bottle and the nuns heated it up in a Burco – I remember all the bottles standing up in this Burco – and you'd go back at lunchtime and get your warm bottle of tea.

I use a small teapot for every day. Whoever makes me tea knows to scald the pot and it takes one teabag in it, and I get a good mug of tea out of it. I hate teabags in a mug. My daughter Sarah is a divil: if she was making tea for four of us, she would put out four mugs and put a teabag in each of them. Her mug says 'Listen carefully, I don't repeat gossip.' I love all those sayings: 'We are not gossiping, we are networking.' I have a cup and inside is written: 'make tea, make a difference.' Another is: 'Where there's tea, there's hope.'

LIL TOBIN

A friend of mine used to tell a bit of a rude story about tea. This fella was going out with a girl who was kind of posh and he was a bit rough. The girl said to him, 'you must come and meet my parents; come for tea on Sunday.' So his sister tried to coach him beforehand, and told

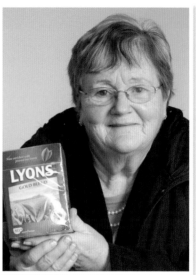

Lil Tobin   Ann Murphy

him to watch his manners and not to eat all around him and to be very polite. So he went along for tea and he was on his best behaviour, saying 'please' and 'thank you', and so on. The lady of the house had this lovely china tea set and the cups had little dogs on the sides. He was holding his cup and saucer and the lady came over to him with the teapot and she said, 'will you have another cup' and he said 'oh no, thank you, Missus, no, no, I'm all right.' But she said, 'oh go on', and just to be sociable, he said 'Oh all right, just fill it up there to the dog's arse.'

ANN MURPHY

My two sons are in Australia. When Padraig went over, I asked him if there was anything he missed from home, and he said 'yes Mammy, Lyons tea'. He said the tea in Australia is terrible. So every fortnight I have to send Lyons tea. Last Friday week, I posted them biscuits and teabags and they had them on the Wednesday in Australia. One son is an electrician and the other is a labourer. There's no work for them

Louie McGrath   Sheila Kearns

here. They are enjoying it and they are about half a mile away from each other in Melbourne, so that helps, but I do miss them. My husband and I visited them for seven weeks and we brought them a good supply of teabags. I thought it was beautiful and please God I'll get to go back again.

LOUIE McGRATH

An old lady once said to me, 'a good dinner deserves a cup of tea after it and a bad dinner needs it.' I love coming to the ALPS group on a Tuesday morning. It gets me out of the house, especially when I'm on my own more or less. It's lovely. It's a great pick-me-up.

SHEILA KEARNS

During war time, the ration was half an ounce of tea per person per week and I remember the ration books so well. When the war was over, my mother gave them to us children to play with, but we didn't want to play with them because we thought they were too precious.

My father always told me that when I was born he had to buy the dearest tea ever. He paid £2 for 2 lb of tea on the black market so that they could make tea for the midwife. Tea was like gold dust but the midwife was always treated like a queen: you just had to have tea for her.

We didn't have a phone, so when the babies were born, my father would have to hire a car to pick up the midwife and bring her back. She lived about six miles away. But the day I was born, in 1942, there were great drifts of snow on the roads so they had to travel in a pony and trap. It took so long that I was born about four hours before she arrived. But she still got her tea.

Catherine O'Neill

Nuala Harte

CATHERINE O'NEILL

I got this teapot in a car boot sale for €5. I absolutely love it. I use it regularly and it has a special place in my kitchen. When I joined ALPS in 1992, my son was only two years old. I joined because I was sitting at home looking at the four walls and it was very lonely. The group had a little nursery and it was great to see my son interacting with other children.

When we made tea for my mother we would put the tea in the teapot and we'd say 'mother, do you want it up to the first nose or the second nose?' The first 'nose' was just under the spout, and meant just one cup of tea – for her, but if it was the second nose then we could get a cup of tea too.

NUALA HARTE

Tea at the Áras

Michael Harte taking tea on a 'car-boot picnic' on a family day trip.

I have a photograph taken at Áras an Uachtaráin, with President McAleese, having the cup of tea. It was about twelve years ago when all the ALPS groups were invited up to the Áras.

I got married forty years ago and Michael got a caravan for our honeymoon. It was my first holiday and his too, and we had a big Morris Oxford car and we pulled the caravan after it and we parked it in Bettystown. The morning after we were married, Michael had to go down to the shop to get tea, sugar, milk, bread, butter and marmalade. I can still see him walking back towards the caravan, carrying the two bags of groceries, smoking a cigar. I can still smell that cigar. That was my first holiday and it was so nice.

We toured around the country after Bettystown, and we parked in Lough Key in County Roscommon. Each day, we used to go into a little tea room called Spellman's. I remember the day we were leaving, Mrs Spellman and a whole lot of children all came out to say goodbye to us and they mentioned us being honeymooners. I asked Michael how they knew we were on honeymoon and he said he didn't know, but it must have been written all over us.

Rosslare Arboreal Day, 1940s.
COURTESY INDEPENDENT NEWSPAPERS IRELAND

CIAN McMAHON

Cian McMahon is chairperson of the Dublin City University Tea Society and deputy station manager with DCU FM.

DCU Tea Society was established in 2012, and now we have over a hundred members. It came about by me making a joke on Twitter. I said if DCU had a tea society, it would have the most relaxing events, and I had about forty replies recommending that I set one up. I didn't think we'd get anyone joining but we ended up with about sixty people signing our constitution and we got ratified by the Students' Union and the Student Life Committee, who oversee society activity at the university. Funnily enough, even though we're an official society, it took us months to get a bank account because the bank doesn't seem to think we could be real. NUI Maynooth and University College Cork have a tea society as well, and we're hoping to organise a meet-up but we'll call it an 'Inter Varsi-tea'. We like puns. Our constitution is filled

A DCU Tea Soc meeting. COURTESY EILEEN STEVENSON

with puns; we actually call it the 'Cons-tea-tution' and I'm officially the 'Tea-seach' of the society.

We have a lot of members who swear they can tell the difference between the major brands of tea, such as Barry's or Lyons, but I've never noticed it. We're hoping to do a taste test, with thirty or forty people, at some stage. Actually, the DCU water isn't very good; it's very hard and overpowers the tea taste, especially if you're making green tea. Last year we ended up spending a lot of money on bottled water, which killed our kettle so now we're trying to track down bottled water that hasn't had minerals added.

We have three glass teapots and each week we try three different types of tea. The two most popular teas are Thé du Hammam and a Darjeeling called 'Margaret's Hope'. People like the Thé du Hammam because it's really fruity and interesting and it smells like sweets. Even people who wouldn't usually like gourmet teas enjoy Margaret's Hope because it's like the perfect cup of Barry's every time. It's hard to mess up. This semester we got four different 'first flushes' – teas made from the very first leaves taken from the trees of that particular year and they're about €50 for 150g. I'm

This semester we got four different 'first flushes' – they're about €50 for 150g.

very interested to try those to see if they're worth the money. That's what the society allows students to do: to try teas that they couldn't afford alone. And there's a lot of chatting and making new friends and meeting people. We also explain the science of making a decent cup of tea, and go into detail about boiling points and such.

People can be very particular about the cup or mug they like. Donal, the president of the Tea Soc, will insist on a bone china cup. The committee of Tea Soc decided to club its own personal money together and order special mugs, from Penny's Pottery on the outskirts of Dingle. They make these beautiful handmade mugs and we had them inscribed with our names and positions.

We're planning themed tea events and talks, such as a Geisha tea ceremony. We also want to find teas from other areas of the world, and even have plans for an 'Irish-themed' tea evening with Barry's and Lyons, and with a sort of 'Irish Mammy' in an apron serving tea and brown bread.

We have a weekly competition which we call the Very Bestest Mug Competition, whereby we decide who has brought the best or coolest mug along to the meeting. The very first one was won by a person who brought in a full tea set, with cup and saucer and teaspoon, the whole lot. Somebody else won it once with a mug that looked exactly like a camera lens. It's great fun.

One committee member – probably the one most into tea – handmade a tea blend for Christmas, and that was really well received. He used cinnamon and nutmeg and spices, and did a workshop on how to blend it. We're now going to get him to make blends for other festivals or occasions such as Valentine's Day. We're not sure what'll go into that one; apparently avocado is an aphrodisiac.

Every year all the clubs and societies have a day where they recruit new members, especially from the first years. So at our stand we got a massive Burco boiler and loads of small shot glasses and provided different samples of tea. Apparently we nearly gave the Students' Union President a heart attack because he thought we were doling out whiskey shots! We also had four types of biscuits – Hobnob, Digestive, Custard

Nate Mc Donald's acrobatic pose won second place in the DCU Tea Soc's photo competition 2013 for the most interesting place to drink tea. COURTESY EIMEAR NÍ FHAOLÁIN

Cream and Rich Tea – and had people guess which one lasted longest for dunking.

Our 2013 Photography Competition asked entrants to take photographs of the most interesting place they can have a cup of tea. Another idea we're working on is called 'Philoso-tea' whereby we have some informal philosophy talks accompanied by tea. We know that a lot of lecturers would be very interested in discussing their topics outside the usual format.

I drink a lot of tea throughout a day. If I'm sitting in front of my computer I'll go through six or seven cups a day. It gives me something to do, if I'm waiting for the computer to perform a task, as well as keep me awake. Tea is so easy to make, it's great. For Christmas I got an amazing little cast iron handmade Japanese teapot. I'll often have that sitting up next to me. It keeps the tea hot forever. We've just bought three of them for the society.

I have always liked tea. Apparently when I was really small – before I had teeth – I used to sit in the People's Park in Dun Laoghaire, gumming Tayto crisps and drinking tea out of a flask; that's what my nanny used to tell me anyway. It doesn't seem like a particularly safe thing to have done, especially for someone without teeth, but I survived.

COLIN STAFFORD JOHNSON

Emmy award-winning cameraman Colin Stafford Johnson has been involved in some of the most highly acclaimed wildlife productions, including his films on tigers in India. Colin presents *Living the Wildlife* on RTÉ. COURTESY CTL FILMS

My tea caddy is one of the few things I have from my original family home. In its early life, of course, it stored tea. I remember so clearly opening up that tea caddy and being hit with the smell of the tea leaves. But later it became a place where I would store my fishing hooks and weights, and sometimes birds' eggs, and even worms for fishing bait; lots of different things have been stored in that tin. It became a handy container that I brought around with me everywhere.

In my early twenties, I took the tea caddy on a trip around the world. I ended up in New Guinea when I was twenty-two. My main reason for being there was because I wanted to see Birds of Paradise and Bowerbirds, birds that had always fascinated me. While I was there, the tea caddy held malaria tablets and antibiotics because that's how I paid my way around. I was travelling in very remote areas where there was no currency, so I traded my way around with medicines. I spent a total of £10 in New Guinea in four months. That area, on the New Guinea and Irian Jaya border (now known as the western island, West Papua) was such a remote place in 1986, it probably held the most remote people on the planet.

In the highlands of New Guinea I met an Australian guy living there, and he had a big box of Lipton teabags, which he had brought with other goodies from Australia, and he packed my tea caddy with these Lipton teabags, the ones with the little strings and the red and yellow labels.

It was amazing because I was heading off into the forest and all I had to eat was what was available, a bit of sweet potato or casaba, and whatever I could get from the local tribal hunter gatherers, who used to hunt for snakes, turtles, tree kangaroos or possums. But in all the madness of living in these places, in the middle of the forest, there was something about being able to sit down, at the end of the day, and have a cup of tea. It somehow kept you in touch with your other life, and there was something very reassuring about having that little tea caddy there with me, a bit like hearing the World Service on a radio.

I was travelling from Mount Wilhelm, the highest point in New Guinea, to the sea, by walking, rafting and canoeing, so it was going to be a four-month trip. After a while I got tired of walking so I made a raft – very badly – so much so that after a mile or two down this river, as I came around this corner the raft hit a load of detritus that had built up across the river, and turned over. I jumped free of the raft and managed to grab my backpack, and I was floating when, in the distance, I saw my tea caddy drifting off down the river. That was one thing I didn't want to lose, so I swam after it, and I retrieved it from the water. Somehow my teabags remained nice and dry inside.

In the distance, I saw my tea caddy drifting off down the river

I was totally lost at that point. I wandered up a little riverbed until I found a place where a tree had been felled across the dry riverbed. I could see that people had been walking across this tree so I decided to try to follow their path because the banks of the river were totally impenetrable. It was difficult to discern the track through the jungle but after about half an hour I came across this little hut on stilts in the forest, with a slippery pole, with notches cut into it to allow you to climb up. So I climbed up the pole and found a group of about fifteen men and women sleeping inside the hut. The walls of this place were lined with bows and arrows and spears. The men were wearing just their penis guards and the women wore grass skirts. There was a little fire smouldering in the room. They made a mud basin on the floor in which they made their fire; they didn't have chimneys, so the smoke just sort of drifted around the room. No sign of the western world at all in that hut, so I thought I'd better not wake them up while they're sleeping because they might never have seen a white man before.

Later on, they woke up and found me outside. We couldn't communicate in any way, and they wouldn't have known what I was doing there or where the hell I'd come from, but that night I ended up sleeping in the hut with them. Their pig got to sleep beside the fire, I got to sleep beside the pig, and the chief got to sleep beside me. So I opened my eyes the next morning to see his face. He had a big bone going through his nasal septum and a little proboscis coming out of the top of his nose, and all sorts of body ornaments.

The next day, the Yapsei River, the tributary of the Sepik I had rafted down, broke its banks and the entire place was flooded so I was stuck there for the time being. The men were bringing in snakes and rats and all sorts of things to cook on the fire, and I had nothing to contribute until I remembered my tea. So I made tea. A hot drink was a completely foreign concept to these people, never mind tea. They suspiciously watched me drink it and then I passed my small plastic cup to the chief. I think they didn't quite know what to think of it, but once one drank it, they all wanted to try it. So the whole tribe tried the tea. As I finished with the teabags, I would drop them down through the slots in the floor of the hut, to the ground below, as they were biodegradable.

The following day I woke up, again with the pig beside me, but I found the chief looking a little different. He had gone down and retrieved all the little red and yellow Lipton tags from the used teabags and put them hanging from his ears. They had become absolute prized possessions, and every time I made a cup of tea he would take off the little tags and add them to his ear collection so by the time I left them he had about twenty hanging from his ears. I called him Mr Lipton, he was a cool guy, but of course we couldn't say a word to each other.

A week later, one of the men was killed on a pig hunt. They came down the Sepik River in their canoe, with this guy who was dying. I was only twenty-two at the time and had no idea what to do. He had had his arm pretty much ripped off by a wild boar. I remember the dugout canoe coming downriver, full of fish scales and blood, and this poor fellow who was dying in front of our eyes. When he died, I couldn't think of what to do, so again, I just started making tea. That was the only thing I could do, just pass around some tea. I was with the tribe until the flood subsided a couple of days later, and then I followed some of the men to another river and they helped me make a raft so we parted ways there.

A missionary told me afterwards that they were probably quite happy to see me leave. They lived on an island in that stretch of forest and had no need to know about the outside world. They wouldn't have wanted me there, but they would have felt responsible for me because I was in their area. They weren't friendly or unfriendly, they just didn't know what I was doing there. But they understood that the tea was a social gesture – they got that. They were giving me something and I was giving them something. My tea caddy is back in my home now, in Wesport, and holds tea once again.

Colin's tea caddy, safely home once more.

There's **more** to enjoy in a **quality** Tea

and that means —

PATTISON'S COLD SEAL TEA

PATTISON'S GOLD SEAL TEA

— it's only 1/10d. a qr. lb.

Oh, for a cup of **PATTISON'S TEA**

"*The Tea with a Tradition*"

Pattison's tea advertisement
Sligo Champion
1958

Tea was even a feature of social events in the Swinging Sixties in Ireland.

MARY CONROY

Mary Conroy is from Kilcullen, in County Kildare, and enjoys knitting, singing and playing the piano.

I love tea. I started drinking tea when I was very young. I was born on 3 September 1940, and I weighed only 3 lb because I was two months premature. Almost all babies were born at home then, with the help of a midwife, and there was no such thing as incubators. I was born with congenital cataracts so I lost my sight. Granny reared me at first because Mammy didn't know how to look after such a small baby and I was her first child. I had to be wrapped in cotton wool. I had my first eye operation when I was six months old and twenty-four operations after that, but if I had had that first operation at three months old, I would have my sight today. Nowadays they know straight away if a baby has cataracts, and they can remove them, but they just didn't know enough back then.

When I make tea for myself it is through touch. I feel the tap and the kettle and put the tea in the pot and fill up the pot with the boiling water. When you pour the tea out, you put your first finger at the top of the cup and when you feel the heat coming towards your finger you take your finger away. You sense the heat.

In later years, they developed little gadgets that helped blind people. If I was boiling water or milk in a saucepan, you put these round glass gadgets, like marbles, in the middle of the saucepan and it bubbles up and makes noise, so you know it's boiling. I had another gadget you could put on the side of the cup instead of using your finger and it used to beep when the water came to the top.

I went to Merrion School for the Blind from the age of seven until I was sixteen. It was a boarding school so I only came home during the holidays. Mammy really didn't want to send me away to school at all, but a local nun came up to the house and gave out to her and said that, for my sake, she couldn't keep me at home. Years later, my sisters told me that Mammy was in a terrible state when I left.

In school, every day at half past four, we had tea and bread and jam, tea was part of the routine. They taught us Braille and music and the usual subjects, too. After school, I worked in a factory in Inchicore in Dublin for thirty years. I was on the factory line packing boxes. You'd get a cup of tea at ten o'clock when you'd go in and then you'd have tea after your lunch and a tea break again at half past four. The tea breaks were a time to relax and chat with people.

Irish people love tea. Tea consoles you and it can calm you. It's a social thing and a break from the work. We used to have a laugh and share stories during the tea break in work. I remember telling them what happened to me one day on my way in to work. I always had to ask someone to help me cross the road. One day, in Inchicore, I could feel someone beside me and I heard high heel shoes on the path. So I said 'Excuse me, would you mind helping me to cross the road?' But they didn't answer me. After a few seconds I realised it wasn't a woman with high heel shoes, because a horse snorted at me. It was a horse walking along on its own. When I went into work I told them I had asked a horse to bring me across the road and they roared laughing! You had to have a sense of humour at times.

Tea consoles you and it can calm you

DUBLIN AIRPORT POLICE/FIRE SERVICE

Each year, a group of firefighters from the Dublin Airport Police/Fire Service take on a challenge for charity. In 2010, a team set out to climb the eighteen highest mountains across the four provinces in just sixty-two hours, taking them through seventeen counties, and travelling a distance of 1,800km. They succeeded in climbing a combined height of 55,400ft, almost twice that of Mount Everest – all in aid of Beaumont Hospital Foundation for Cancer Treatment. In 2011, the firefighters rowed their 25ft Celtic longboat from Howth to Holyhead, 100km, in just twelve hours, to raise funds for the 3Ts: Turn the Tide of Suicide. For more information on the APFS charity work, see www.firefighterschallenge.ie

MICK GURLEY

Mick Gurley is a paramedic with Police/Fire Service in Dublin Airport.
COURTESY GER TREHY

I like strong tea with a drop of milk. I am very unfussy about cups or mugs. I drink two to three cups per day. I like Lyons Gold Blend.

In training, I also drink a lot of water and green tea. My son is fourteen and he drinks tea with no milk. He plays football so I said to him, 'it's not a big step for you to drink green tea.' I was drinking camomile tea at the time so I said, 'just smell it, you might like it.' He said to me 'Dad, that smells like a pet shop.' So I gave up, but I had a little sniff of it myself, and I thought, 'he's actually right.'

In the Rowing Club we set ourselves challenges for charity and we also do races. We've done the rowing race around Ireland's Eye, and

The APFS Rowing team on their 25ft Celtic longboat, during the Celtic Challenge in 2012 (160km from Arklow to Aberystwyth, Wales) in aid of Barretstown.

(L–r): Eamon Griffin or 'The Elder'; Ken 'Gomez' Gorman, Declan 'Suede' Egan, and Mick Gurley, a 'paramatey', in their kitchen at Dublin Airport Fire Station.

the Ocean to City Race in Cork, and down the River Barrow. We won the Barrow race twice so that's going well. Next we're hoping to row the length of the River Shannon in three days, 320km from Lough Allen to Shannon Airport. During a challenge, your hydration is all important, to keep your electrolytes right, so you're drinking sports drinks and carbohydrate powders. Now we all know tea is a diuretic, so that's not good. But yet there are times when you just have to have a cup of tea. I don't know what it is.

We took part in the Celtic Challenge race in 2012, and when we were rowing across the Irish Sea, we experienced the worst weather conditions in all the years they've run the Challenge. The boat was being thrown around and people were getting sick. We took shifts rowing and when you got a break, you would get onto the support yacht that was following us. You had to go downstairs to make tea. Because you're still getting your sea legs, you don't like being down

There are times when you just have to have a cup of tea

below, because you lose sight of the horizon, so you're disorientated. I think it took me twenty-five minutes to make a cup of tea. I remember one of the lads, Eamon, looking at me, thinking there was something wrong with me and that I was about to collapse, because it took me so long to make this cup of tea.

Despite the ease and safety of just sitting up on deck and opening a bottle of water or an energy drink, during the short break from rowing, you would spend great time and effort in a nauseating cabin – being thrown around by rough seas, and struggling with boiling water – all for the sake of a cup of tea. When I did eventually manage to crawl back on deck, and found a little corner where I could drink my tea, it really did hit the spot. It might not be good for the body, but it's good for the soul.

The APFS team climbing Mount Errigal, Donegal, in 2010 for the Beaumont Foundation.
COURTESY APFS CHALLENGE TEAM

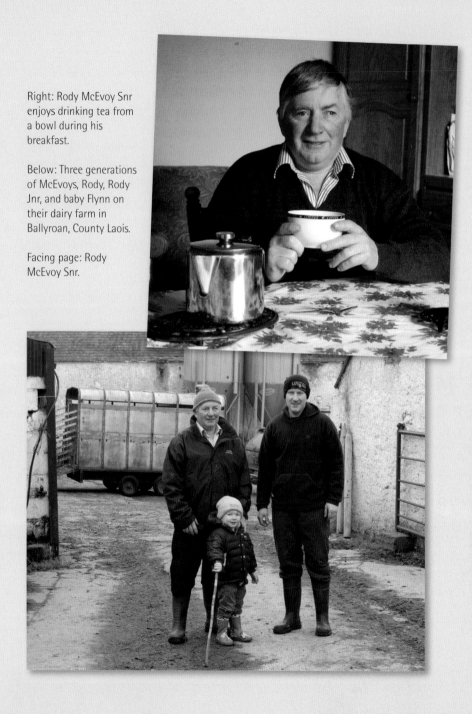

Right: Rody McEvoy Snr enjoys drinking tea from a bowl during his breakfast.

Below: Three generations of McEvoys, Rody, Rody Jnr, and baby Flynn on their dairy farm in Ballyroan, County Laois.

Facing page: Rody McEvoy Snr.

RODDY COLLINS

Roddy Collins is a football manager and former professional footballer, who has won the League of Ireland title and FAI Cup with Bohemians FC. He is also a radio and television pundit.

My first memory of tea is from my granny's house, when I was about eight years old. She lived off Harrington Street on Dublin's South Circular Road, and we used to go over on the bus to visit her. She had a small little parlour, and my mother, my two aunties Marie and Sheila and my granny would sit around the fire there drinking tea, while we played. My granny would always look into the cup, staring at the tea leaves, and she'd say, 'Jesus, I see a big tall dark handsome man', and the man always had a herringbone overcoat for some reason. My aunts were single and they loved hearing about the tall dark man. 'He looks like a film star,' my granny would say, 'a big shock of black hair on his head, and he's coming across the sea.' Then the next week it would be 'oh there's going to be a tragedy', and my ma and aunties would shout: 'I don't want to know about that one!' Growing up, I thought that my granny was actually a fortune teller, but nothing she predicted ever happened.

When I was thirteen or fourteen, on the bus to school in the mornings, two or three of us would stay on the bus and we'd head up to Arnotts, and we'd go up the big double wrought-iron stairs in Arnotts, and we'd sit down up there and order a pot of tea and a scone, to start the day, like aul' ones. And we had no money, so if anyone left a half a scone on the next table or a tip, we'd take that too, and order another pot. It was very innocent when you think about it – going for tea in Arnotts. If you're going to mitch from school, don't go near Arnotts. All my uncles and aunts would be in there, so I was caught loads of times. We'd be sitting there with our scones and tea, like royalty.

My daughter is a schoolteacher and she asked me recently why I never wanted to go to school. I went to a Christian Brothers school and we were physically bashed every day so that's why we didn't want to go to school. I came from Cabra and our father tried to better us so he sent us to that school, while all my mates went to the local tech. My poor father thought he was progressing us, and he was unintentionally doing the opposite. They singled us out because of where we came from. They knew we were grateful to be there and they took advantage of that – with a big leather strap.

When you got on the bus in the morning you'd feel physically sick. So a lot of the time we just couldn't face it when the bus stopped at the school, but you had to put in a lot of hours, hanging around town, sitting in Stephen's Green. It wasn't great craic at all.

As I got older I worked on the building sites, and tea is very important on the building sites. I remember working over on Morehampton Road in one of the big houses, and the lady of the house was a real toff, so we weren't allowed into her house. We had to sit out on the steps and she'd give you out a cup of tea and in winter, by the time you'd put the cup down on the step, it would be freezing. That was the first time I had 'iced' tea.

When I started as a kid on the sites, we used to make the tea in a billycan and you'd put a stick into it to stop the smoke getting in. Some days you might only get half an hour for your lunch so if any part of it wasn't done right – if the teaboy or the nipper didn't get the can boiling to brew the tea, or the stick wasn't in – it was a disaster for everyone. I was a plasterer, and you'd be working hard from 8 a.m. so when you sat down to have a cup of tea if it wasn't right, everyone would be giving out and the day was ruined.

Everything that happened in our house was marked with a cup of tea. I remember when I was about twenty, I had to go and talk to my father about something serious. He was building an extension on the back of the house at the time, and he was up putting on a roof. I said 'Da, I've something to tell you. I'm dreading telling you this', and he said 'What is it?', and I told him and straight away he shouted in to my mother: 'Collette, put the tea on.' We sat down to talk about sorting this out and discussing what to do and what not to do, and another pot of tea was put on. Suddenly there were six of us sitting round the table having a pot of tea, all sorting out the one problem.

Tea is huge in soccer. The first thing I'll do in any new club is organise a Burco boiler. It's really important for the boys when they come in; the tea allows them to pause and have a chat. It's just a tradition. I played in England and when you went in for training every morning there was always a big pot of tea on the table. It was made with leaves and the cups would be laid out and all the lads would come in for the cup of tea. When training was over we'd all have another cup of tea.

A cup of tea is a great drink to cool you down and stop you sweating. I worked out in Malta as a football manager and I had to wear a shirt and tie for all the meetings, and I would be melting in the heat, while the others would be fine. I once asked the president of the club, 'How come I'm sweating and I'm drinking cold water, and you're all drinking tea and you're fine?' He said 'Rod, it's a cup of green tea you need; it heats up the core of your body and takes down your temperature.' And he was right. I remember a team from Ireland came out to play a team from Valletta, and I said to the manager: 'After training give the lads a pot of green tea.' 'Are you for real, Rod?' he said, 'It's forty degrees out there.' I told him to trust me. The minute they came in at half time he gave them all hot tea, and by the time they went back out they were all grand again.

> *It's a cup of green tea you need; it heats up the core of your body and takes down your temperature.*

Hospitality is very important to Irish people. You'd often hear people giving out about homes they visit: 'They never even gave us a cup of tea, the miserable swines, not even a cup of tea.'

My wife's mother, who lived in the flats in O'Devaney Gardens, always had a pot of tea on the go, from morning to bedtime. I remember when she moved from her flat into a house, her new kitchen was her pride and joy. She had nine children, and that meant nine boyfriends and girlfriends and whoever else might call, and everyone would have to have a cup of tea. 'You'll have a cup of tea', you'd be told, and you'd have to say, 'I'd love one, Mrs Hanney, thanks' and she'd always make sure to give you something to eat with it. But I always remember on the very, very rare occasion she didn't like someone, she'd laugh and say: 'give them a hard chair and a cold cup of tea and they won't be around for long.'

JOHN McAREAVEY

John's wife, Michaela McAreavey, departed this world in January 2011. Through the Michaela Foundation, John and the Harte family want to commemorate and celebrate Michaela's life. For more information about the work of the foundation, please see www.themichaelafoundation.com

From 2003 to 2007, I studied at Queens University in Belfast, and I lived in an area between Queens and the Ormeau Road called the 'Holy Lands' due to the local street names, such as Palestine Street and Jerusalem Street. It's a massive student area, where all the students stay during term time, and a brilliant place to live. I always described it as a big playpen. Michaela and her three friends lived in a house there, right in the centre of the Holy Lands, and Michaela and her best friend, Edel, were pioneers. After a night out, all their friends would come back down to the Holy Lands and almost anyone who arrived at their door would be let in, but you wouldn't get anything stronger than tea there, and maybe toast and biscuits. I think Edel and Michaela liked this idea: that they might be sobering a few people up before they headed on home.

JOHN McAREAVEY | 179

I actually got to know Michaela through the tea house. We went there one night with a couple of her friends, to a sort of 'after-party'. I remember there was just tea everywhere, and because there was no alcohol, things never got messy. It was just nice to be able to sit and get a cup of tea at two o'clock in the morning.

That's how it developed – everybody started to refer to their house as the 'tea house', and the girls loved it. They were in that house for two years so for two years random students met there. There's a huge Gaelic culture down there so it was through friends of friends – word of mouth – that people would hear about the tea house, and I think the girls liked meeting new people. If you were from Derry or Down or Fermanagh, they would discover some kind of link or someone in common, and then you'd be in. So any time we went out, we would always go back to the house afterwards and have tea, and it was always brilliant craic. Sometimes people would bring along a guitar and there would be a sing-song and this could go on until four or five in the morning.

Even though Michaela and Edel didn't drink, they were always full of craic. If I wasn't taking a drink, I wouldn't be looking to stay up all hours, but they would be still so lively in the middle of the morning. They just didn't need alcohol.

When I first started to go out with Michaela, and before people knew we were a couple, I remember nights sitting in the tea house until seven or eight in the morning, because we were waiting to get a bit of 'alone time', to have a wee court, but people wouldn't leave. It's funny, one time a good friend of mine came down to go out and he didn't know about me and Michaela – the romantic angle – he just thought we were friends, but didn't he come back to the house with all of us and he was the last one to leave, after drinking seven cups of tea. Michaela kept on offering him tea, because he kept on drinking it. She didn't want to be rude, so he ended up leaving at seven in the morning. I still slag him about that now. Seven cups of tea!

But that's what she was like: she was a really good host. She probably got it from her own house. The Hartes are all big tea drinkers.

In fact, we never had a biccie drawer in my family's house until Michaela came along. We wouldn't have been big tea people, except for my mum who drinks tea on tap, throughout the day, but it was Michaela who really introduced us to the joy of tea and buns and cakes. Mum loved this because she's a great baker, and because Michaela had such a sweet tooth, together they could enjoy tea and apple pie and meringues and all sorts. It just became a real social activity in our home.

Michaela always brought a wee flask of tea to GAA matches, and her biscuits. I never saw someone so into tea at such a young age, yet she wasn't at all old fashioned. She was very close to her granny and she loved going over to her granny's for tea, the social side of it. Tea was a massive part of our lives and Michaela's life. The tea house became a kind of social hub in the middle of the Holy Lands, an oasis of tea drinking and craic and sobriety at the same time. It was unique for students.

We're hoping to build the Michaela Foundation Centre up in Tyrone, and from the beginning we knew it had to include a café that would be themed around the tea house, and in fact, it will be called the Tea House. Indeed, I would love, in the future, as another activity for the foundation, to encourage students in various campuses to consider the tea house – just to suggest the idea that you can go out and

the Tea house

Flatmates at the 'tea house' (l–r): Kate Frizelle, Michaela, Edel McCarron and Gemma Corey.

COURTESY JOHN McAREAVEY

you don't have to get blind drunk, you can still enjoy yourself and you can still come back and have a cup of tea together.

In Spain and France you can go into coffee shops at eleven and twelve o'clock at night, and I love that idea, but here you have to go to a pub and that means you're drinking. It would be great if it wasn't just exclusively alcohol at night, if there was another option. Really it's about creating a culture. It's not even about the tea; it's about sitting around and sharing stories. It is amazing.

Nowadays if you go into a café or a bar during the day and you look around at the groups of young people, they'll all be sitting bent over mobile phones, and on laptops, all separate from each other. And yet Irish people are renowned for sharing stories. People are going to start to lose that skill of conversation. They can't look at someone – they'd rather live their lives through their online perspective and how they'd like to be presented, but they can't look at you and talk to you. It would be great to encourage a new social connection for people.

Because Michaela and I had such fun in university, the Michaela Foundation has created a Student Awards Scheme and last year we awarded three first year students starting university with a £1,000 bursary: one who was studying Irish and one studying Religious Education, because they were the two subjects Michaela taught, and then one from a general discipline. This year we're going to award at least six bursaries.

For the younger age group, we piloted the Michaela Girls Summer Camp in Tyrone in July 2012 for seventy girls, aged from eleven to thirteen. We are trying to encourage the idea of having the strength to be yourself, and we chose five core elements which Michaela really held dear in her life: Fun, Faith, Fashion, Irish and

Michaela McAreavey.
COURTESY JOHN McAREAVEY

Wellbeing. We planned a timetable of events around those five key elements. It lasted one week and the girls just absolutely loved it. We never expected such a reaction. It was amazing and even the volunteers got so much out of it. You'd see the girls blossom through the week. During the summer in Ireland there are lots of camps, but they're usually sports related. So what happens if you're not into sports? There should be alternatives. These young girls and their parents sent us letters and gave us such wonderful feedback, which was really, really heartening. This year we're hoping to run ten camps throughout Ireland, and the long-term aim is to have a summer camp in every county in Ireland.

As a charity, the Michaela Foundation is in its infancy, but we're feeling our way and people have been so willing to fund-raise for us, it has been great. And on a personal level it's been good for me too to be able to focus on something so positive.

I'm in the fortunate position that I have a strong faith and I know where Michaela is and it's allowed me to focus on the positive. People will probably never forget what happened to Michaela but hopefully through the foundation, we can show all the positive sides to her life. You look at what you've lost but I had such a brilliant time with Michaela

Everybody who knew Michaela seemed to be really touched by her

and everybody who knew Michaela seemed to be really touched by her, she was just such a positive person. Her spirit always shone through.

Harvest scene at Wilton, Cork in late July 1947.

ELSIE HERAGHTY

Elsie Heraghty, from Circular Road, Sligo, passed away on 19 March 2013. A truly wonderful, warm and funny lady, Elsie was famous for her hospitality and great kindness to all her family and friends, and her little dog, Pippa.

I have a set of delph and the sugar bowl looks the exact same as the cup, except for the lack of a handle of course. I was having tea one day with my grand-niece Judith and my daughter Geraldine, and I used this set. I poured the tea for Judith and she proceeded to drink her tea and we had a chat. It was only when she was finished and I was about to pour her a second cup that Geraldine noticed that I had given Judith the sugar bowl. We had such a laugh over that. She didn't want to mention that her cup had no handle. But it's actually happened three times since then with this set of delph and it always seems to happen when the visitor is someone I'd like to be exact about! I always ended up giving them the sugar bowl. The result was I had to hide the sugar bowl away in another press.

I'm eighty-eight years old and I have seen so much change, I can't believe it. The world has changed so much and people have changed. When I was young, you could trust people. We could trust the gardaí, teachers, doctors and lots of people like that, and you looked up to them all, and we thought we could trust the priests. But there's no respect for anyone now. I find that difficult. I often tell my grandsons that years ago if you went down town, everyone saluted you and men lifted their hats to you. People don't know what that is now.

You go down town now and you wouldn't meet anyone you know. Everyone is a stranger. I've no neighbours left now. We all moved in here sixty years ago, and we're all about the same age. There are only three of us left now on Circular Road. These were the first houses to be built in Sligo after the war. When we moved into these houses, we had all just gotten married, and all the children were reared together. We used to be in and out of each other's houses for cups of tea. If my child did something wrong and my next-door neighbour chastised them, you left it. There was never a bad word between us. The parents and children all got on well. Of course the children fought with each other at times, but then they'd be friends again. And teachers nowadays aren't allowed look sideways at the children. I don't know what way things will go in the future.

My daughter Geraldine only drinks green tea. I hate it. She brings her own green teabags with her when she visits. I like nice tea, Lyons Red Label. My mother was always drinking tea. As teenage girls we were always in and out of the house and we used to tease her for drinking too much tea and she'd say 'I'm not making tea now, I'm making starch.' Back then everyone starched their pillowcases and tablecloths – you never see that now. Whether she was making starch or not, the kettle was always on.

My older brother Jim was in England when the war started. He was a fitter in an aircraft factory in Surrey. When Jim heard that the war was coming he bought my mother a big wooden tea chest because he knew it would be rationed and he knew Mammy had to have her tea. He sent home the tea chest and it was put up in the loft and she'd still buy her rations of tea, a half ounce per person per week, and there were a good few children – seven – in our house at that time, so she'd get four and a half ounces, but we were all given cocoa. And then cocoa got scarce so all we had was cocoa shell, which was horrible. My mother always said the tea was bad for children.

The big wooden tea chest was lined with tin foil. She had a tea caddy and when it ran out you'd have to go up to the loft and fill it up for her. That tea chest, along with the rations, lasted us all through the war. We bought the rations every week and the bit extra came from the loft. Tea was awfully important to my mother, she'd have died without her tea. There used to a rhyme about the rations, but I can't remember it exactly, but it was about two ounces of tea and the brown bread. I remember the first white loaf we ever saw. After being so many years with just this brown bread that tasted like sawdust, this first white loaf we got was left sitting on the table, and we all sat and stared at it.

I don't take tea too strong, and I take just a drop of milk. I don't really like milk. Every morning for my breakfast, I just have a cup of tea and a slice of toast and a yogurt. I've always been very active, I ran and raced around here all my life. I get mad with myself when I can't do the things I used to do. I'd get up in the morning and paint a room and it wouldn't knock a fog out of me, and I used to do all the gardening and keep the flowers nice and now I just look out at it, because the stooping kills me. It's hard when your mind is right, to realise you can't do the same things. Mentally you're still a young girl!

My husband Jack passed away thirty-five years ago. I would never have dreamed of getting married again. I suppose we were brought up to be independent women so you got on with things. I am very lucky to have had three lovely children, two wonderful boys and a girl. I have eight grandsons, and now even two great grandchildren. So I've been very blessed. I've had a great, long, happy life.

JOHN JOE McBREARTY

Aged sixty and still loving his tea, John Joe McBrearty is a musician and radio presenter from Kilcar, County Donegal.

'Tae, tae, tae, don't heed the rations!' was an old saying around Kilcar in the 1950s and 1960s that came from the war times.

I gave up milk and sugar for Lent about three years ago, and never went back. But my wife always drank her tea black. I drink a lot of tea now. I liked 'Donegal tea', which used to be made in a factory in Kilcar.

I started drinking tea when I was very young. I remember when I was five or six, I used to go and help my aunt with the hay in the

Tae, tae, tae, don't heed the rations!

summer time. Their hay was on a bank that ran down to the shore. I remember I used to love when they stopped to make the tae. I used to be waiting for that. I used to love the tea – it tasted so different out beside the seaside. I don't know why it was so nice. You would go back up to the house afterwards and have tea and it wouldn't be the same.

And I used to love bog tea as well, and it would be steaming away all day, and it would be like tar by evening and still you would take it. Mind you, the tea in my mother's house was the same. Because we had a shop, the teapot was on the fire all day, and it would be black, but she'd still keep pouring the tea all day.

I remember having a lovely cup of tea in the dressing room before appearing on *The Late Late Show* with my band, Pluto, in the 1970s.

We bring teabags abroad with us if we're going away. Even if we're going down the country, my wife would bring a few teabags in case there were none in the hotel room.

I'll be killed for telling this story. Years ago, when I was away on holidays with the wife, I kept a diary about all the places we went and all the things we did. A year or two later, back home, my wife read that diary. As she read it, she was saying 'that was a great holiday' and 'oh remember that day, wasn't that a lovely trip?' And then after a while, she says: 'Why have you written down "tea" on this day?' And on the next page, 'we had a queer cup of tea today' or 'good cup of tea' on another day. She said she didn't remember the tea. I said, 'do you not remember the cups of tea that we had?' Then I started laughing and the penny dropped. She understood the code I had used. We're married twenty-five years, but she's going to kill me for telling this story in an interview!

JUANITA BROWNE

Juanita Browne, author of this book.

It's only fair that I attempt to answer the same questions I asked so many people during the course of writing this book. So here goes:

Sweet tea memories

One of my earliest tea memories is of my granny pouring tea from her little silver teapot. I can clearly remember the engraved design, the small dent on one side, and its black plastic handle. It held only about two cups of tea, and she always used tea leaves. My granny lived next door so we spent a lot of time in her house. She crocheted her own tea cosies and tablecloths and I now realise she was a master of a beautiful old Irish lace crochet technique that has all but disappeared. She also had a great talent for crosswords, whist, growing plants and raising orphaned wild animals of any kind. And she regularly made me tea when I was small. I would sit at her kitchen table and Gang-gann would make me laugh with her stories and rhymes and advice, and pour her strong tea.

I have had so many great chats over tea with my close friends through school, college and working life. Tea is also, of course, the great friend of the procrastinator. Studying or work has always been punctuated by cups of tea. Even while working on this book, there was usually a cup of tea beside my laptop. I also find myself carrying cups around the house. I once discovered a half-empty cup of tea in the hot press. Well, one must quench one's thirst when folding one's clothes.

I have such nice memories of sitting around my mother's kitchen table. There were four girls and one boy in my family and we spent a lot of time sitting around that table, drinking tea and chatting. It has always been the centre of the household, and when people visited the house, tea would be made straight away.

Of course, like most people, I have also experienced sad occasions that were accompanied by tea. When my sister Elaine died in 2008, we all stayed up very late, making pots and pots of tea, because we didn't know what else to do. It was almost automatic, a way of getting through those awful first hours of horror and shock. You know you won't be able to sleep because your world has fallen apart, so you make tea. It's actually too early and too raw to say much to each other, so rather than sitting silently, you can make tea together, and there's something comforting in that. I can't imagine those early days without the comfort of tea and more importantly the action of making tea for people.

Tea, shoots and leaves

My own tea recipe would be: medium strength, generous milk and very, very hot. My favourite tea is now Barry's, despite growing up in a Lyons house. My mother always bought Lyons Green Label. I remember so clearly the torn Lyons car draw tokens piled up on the little shelf where she keeps her tea caddy. It was my husband, Joe, who led me to Barry's, as he came from a Barry's household. So it was a mixed marriage. During those early trips to the supermarket, I found myself faced with this massive life-changing decision – do I cut my tea ties with my own family? I may have felt just a little disloyal but I did convert to Barry's. I think my family know I still love them.

My favourite cup

Despite owning some nice mugs and even some pretty cups and saucers, I usually find myself reaching for this dull, unattractive mug I bought in a shop that sold remnants and damaged kitchen goods, when I was a poor student (unlike now, when I'm ... no longer a student). It's a dark blue mug with a sickly mustard colour on the inside. I don't actually like how it looks, but it keeps the tea hot and I love the taste of tea from it. I'm pretty sure it's not all in my imagination.

But then there is also my second favourite mug – an amazing tea-drinking vessel brought to me all the way from Bavaria by my good friend Caroline Rattenhuber. At first it seems like just an ordinary run-of-the-mill black mug, but then, when you're least expecting it, you pour your tea, and as if by magic, the fairytale scene of Neuschwanstein Castle (which inspired Walt Disney's Sleeping Beauty castle) reveals itself. Of course, mugs are a great present, because it's nice to think of a good friend over a cup of tea, and this one reminds me of Caroline, drinking fancy fruit tea in Germany while I have mine in Kildare.

Tea infused with fresh air

Many people have mentioned the joy of tea in the great outdoors. I share their enthusiasm for hot tea in the wilds – especially in Ireland's often inhospitable conditions. One memorable outdoor cup of tea was enjoyed on the banks of Lough Ree last year, during a complicated film shoot of whooper swans for a wildlife documentary on the River Shannon. It was mid-January and after a 5 a.m. start we were running

Tea is an absolute necessity on those early mornings with small children. Juanita with her two boys, Ben (six) and John (three).

around, in and out of boats and vans, for about ten hours before we were able to take a break. We had two large flasks of tea, with their two plastic cups, but we had forgotten to bring extra cups, and there were about eight of us. We proceeded to take turns having a cup of tea, and shared around those life-saving plastic cups of goodness. In those freezing conditions, when you're wet, cold, and tired, it is so welcome. That was one of the best cups of tea I ever tasted.

My most important cup of tea

My most important cup of tea is that life-saving cup first thing in the morning. My first baby decided not to waste his early years sleeping. He believed sunrise was a great time to make a start on the day. I'm a complete night owl, not a morning person at all. So, each day, I would lie in bed for a few minutes, watching the clock blink 5.05 a.m., and I would think, 'how will I possibly get out of bed, never mind make it through a whole day minding a non-napping newborn?' I would hobble downstairs, babe in arms, and the first thing I would do is put on the kettle. Somehow, miraculously, after that first cup of tea, I'd feel able to face the day. In fact, perhaps it was my gratitude to those early morning mugs of tea that made me want to write this book; thank you, tea!

Now, why don't we go and put the kettle on?

Thompson's Restaurant and Ca...

The finest and most comfortable in the South of Ireland

SPECIAL QUALITY

TRADE MARK REGISTERED

"The Capital Tea"

HALF POUND NET

STR... AND FL...

Willi...
and
12-16
D...

BUY

"Globo Tea" — FOR HEALTH AND ECONOMY

SOLD ALL OVER THE GLOBE

RED SEAL 3/-

"GLOBO" TEA

PRICES PER LB.

GREEN SEAL	2/-
BROWN SEAL	2/4
BLUE SEAL	2/8
RED SEAL	3/-
GOLD SEAL	4/-

WHOLESALE:
COYLE LTD.
30 UPPER ABBEY STREET
DUBLIN, C.9

Whole...
and S...

Win...
S...

Bran...

Blended

0d. 1/-, 1/4, 1/6, 1/...
2/2, 2/4, 2/6, 2/10, 3/...
and 3/2

CHINA TEAS—2/8 and

Oh, for
a cup
of

PATTISO
T...

"The Tea with a Tradition"

Becker Bros., Ltd.

8 South Gt. George's Street
and 17 North Earl Street,
DUBLIN

Estd. 1867

Telephone 21172

"The Capital Tea"

HALF POUND NET

SPE...